BIRTHDAY PARTIES

Vicki Lansky

MJF BOOKS

NEW YORK

14133383

Editorial thanks to: Kathryn Ring, Sandra Whelan, Theresa Early, Julie Surma, Kate Moore, Cindy Shellum and Francie Paper.
Also thanks to: The Deephaven Montessori School, Nancy Wiederhold, Linda Moorhead, Mary McNamara, and Linda Wiegel.

Illustrations: Jack Lindstrom
Cover Design and Art Direction: MacLean & Tuminelly

Published by MJF Books
Fine Communications
Two Lincoln Square
60 West 66th Street
New York, NY 10023

Birthday Parties: Best Party Tips and Ideas

ISBN 1-56731-323-X

Special thanks to the parents who shared their words and feelings. Their quotes are reprinted with permission from Vicki Lansky's *Practical Parenting*™ newsletter.

Manufactured in the United States of America on acid-free paper
MJF Books and the MJF colophon are trademarks of Fine Creative Media, Inc.

10   9   8   7   6   5   4   3   2   1

Table of Contents

Introduction

Who, Me, Give a Party?

Yes, you can give a wonderful birthday party for your young child that is as much fun for you as for the birthday child and the guests. These younger years are a very special time. By the time kids are in elementary school they have very definite ideas about their own parties—which might not coincide with yours. This is a chance to focus on your child and create memories that will last a lifetime. Besides, birthday parties are a tremendous boost to any child's self-esteem. A happy day of one's own is the best birthday gift you can give your child.

The basic components of any party are really quite simple: invitations, decorations, presents, cake and ice cream, favors, and some planned activities. Don't try to include every idea you've ever heard or read about *(that includes the ideas in this book, too!)* or you'll be exhausted and the kids will be overwhelmed. Give the kind of party you enjoy giving—not the one you think you "should" give. Too often, parents look upon a birthday party as a ritual to be endured, or as an opportunity to make a lavish party for their own friends.

For young children, these are the best rules to follow:

KEEP IT SMALL

KEEP IT SHORT

KEEP IT SIMPLE

KEEP IT MOVING

AND KEEP YOUR SENSE OF HUMOR !

Where Do I Start?
Getting Organized

Successful birthday parties don't happen by magic; the good ones are planned. It's important to bear in mind that any child's birthday party, after the first one, is for him or her, not for you. Forget showing off either your child or your decorating talents. A party must be fun for your child and the guests. Keeping it manageable, yet flexible, is the secret of success. And planning is the key!

You can plan in your head, but most of us need to put our plans and ideas down on paper. Provided here and throughout the book are checklists you can photocopy and use as you plan your party. Or they may simply provide you with some thoughts as you make your own lists.

You are going to need to consider:

__ Invitations   __ Other food
__ Decorations   __ Paper supplies
__ Favors   __ Camera and film
__ Prizes, if any   __ Party area/location
__ Cake   __ Activities
__ Ice cream   __ Supplies for activities

Budget Considerations

Even the simplest birthday parties cost money. What you should spend is only what you can afford to spend. Obviously, the more you create from scratch, the less the party will cost.

• A good way to save money is not to serve a meal. Cake and ice cream are the main components of any party, and if you provide those, you will really have done it all.

• Activities away from home that carry a high price tag can be offset by limiting the number of guests.

• Spending to compete with your neighbors will be something only you are aware of—your child won't—at least not for several more years.

Age Considerations

Considering what your child is ready for at his or her specific age will go a long way to helping you plan a successful day. Your attitude and expectations can make a big difference in how well any party goes. Children grow and change dramatically from year to year, so you need to rethink your approach for each birthday.

Age 1

Ones have absolutely no concept of parties, despite the significance of the occasion. Schedules and formal games are unnecessary. But since the first birthday is such a landmark, it has a section all its own in Chapter 4. Keep the party short: ½ to 1 hour will more than suffice.

Age 2

Twos are demanding, possessive, and grabby and can't truly grasp the idea of a party. Parties need to be planned with their social immaturity in mind, and with their parent(s) included. A party with a few favorite adults can be just as satisfying for a 2-year-old. as one with two or three other children. Supervised parallel play and a few activities will occupy a child of 2 and a few friends. Remember that small children have small attention spans.

No 2-year-old. remembers a first birthday party, so whatever you do will be new and exciting. A party for this age need only be 1 to 1½ hours long.

Age 3

Children of 3 and up usually love a party. Those who are used to group situations can usually handle a party very well. If your child is shy or a loner, keep that in mind when setting up your party plan. While some children will be happy to stay at your house without a parent, some will not. Keep the party fairly informal. Avoid loud, rough games which may overstimulate children at this age. Separate quarreling children; it is better to remove a difficult child than to punish the child—after all, this is a party. 3-year-olds will enjoy both group games and solitary play. For the most part do not expect this age to cooperate in playing group games. Limit yourself to one or two, as too many group games can overwhelm them. They will happily take part in art projects, singing and circle activities. Some may need to sit alone and play with an assortment of unbreakable toys from the birthday child's collection. Guests of this age have been known to want to take their own gifts home with them, so don't be surprised if you have to deal with behavior problems. Between 1 and 2 hours should be enough time for the children and for you.

Age 4

Children of 4 understand the idea of a birthday party just for them and really appreciate it and get excited about it. Discipline is usually not a problem at this age. Still, speed and simplicity are in order. You will need short games, and you must keep the party moving because 4-year-olds find it hard to wait their turn. Hunts of all kinds work well for this age and up. A good story, simple arts and crafts projects, and games will all be enjoyed. Physical energy abounds, so plan to channel it. Party time of 1½ hours, but not more than 2½ hours, will work well.

Age 5

Children of 5 feel that parties are important and sometimes enjoy the planning and the anticipation even more than the party itself. While children of this age may seem self-contained and capable, the highly charged atmosphere of a party can be hard for a 5-year-old. to handle. Theme party ideas work well with this age. It is still hard for children of 5 to take turns, and they will need to be entertained steadily. Same-sex parties start to emerge for some at this age. Be sure to mark guests' take-home items clearly, because 4-year-olds don't like to "lose" things or get their possessions mixed up with others'. Parties away from home can work, but you still run the risk of overwhelming your child and/or the guests. Be conservative in the place you pick and the number of guests you invite if you'll be outside the house. The ideal length of parties for this age is about 2 hours.

Age 6 and up

Elementary-age children love parties, love the traditions, and eagerly plan and participate in all of it. A sense of fairness will be evident; theme parties are enjoyed; fewer children are fussy eaters. Their exuberance requires you to be well-organized. Parties away from home can work well from this age and on. Children at this age begin have their own ideas of how they want their party to be run. Do listen to them. After all, it's their day! Parties of 2 to 2½ hours are fine. Parties for 6 to 8-year olds should not exceed 3 hours, or the children will get tired, overexcited, and hard to handle.

Choosing the Date

Plan the party for a day that's convenient for you, one when you'll have adequate help. Weekends are better, for example, if you want help from your spouse or a school-age sitter.

• Try to set the party date for the actual birthday, but don't be rigid about it. Kids don't care that much. However, if the party isn't on the child's birthday, you will probably find yourself celebrating twice!

• If your child's birthday falls on a holiday, remember that potential guests may have other plans. Send out invitations extra early, or consider having the party another day.

• Take school schedules into account. If some of the children are in kindergarten, both morning and afternoon may be out, and both kindergarten and nursery school children may be too tired to enjoy a party on a school day. If the birthday is on a school day and you decide to save the celebration for the weekend, you can still make the birthday special by having your child take some treats to school to share with friends.

• Don't hesitate to call parents to check on the schedules of best friends without whom the party won't be a success.

My husband, a dentist, confessed that he believed for some years that all our children had been born on Wednesday until he realized that Wednesday happened to be his day off.
Betty James, New London, CT

Choosing the Hours

• Consider morning, afternoon, and early evening hours. Aim for the time that best suits your child's schedule, and keep in mind that some children take naps, even if yours doesn't. Late morning on a Saturday may be your best choice if you have to work around naps and schedules. If you're past nap-taking age, and if you're not serving a meal, 1 to 3 P.M. can be ideal—after lunch and early enough so dinner won't be spoiled.

• Don't try to make a marathon of the party and a martyr of yourself. Exceptions to the brief party rule may be extra time for a party held at a picnic ground, skating rink, or some other away-from-home place, and an extra half-hour for a party at which a full meal is served.

• Do plan the end of the party as well as the beginning. If you're worried that some parents may not pick up their children on time, plan to take them home yourself so the party will end on your time schedule.

• Evening parties are the worst. Kids are too tired!

Making Up the Guest List

Although parties and crowds may go hand in hand for adults, this is not the case for little children. A large party, even if all the children know each other, can be overwhelming for you as well as for the kids. If you really want to include every member of your child's preschool class, send the treats and favors to school. Don't invite everyone to your home. For those not invited (neighbors, cousins, aunts and uncles), save a piece of birthday cake or a balloon to share with them later.

If the children are 1 or 2 years old, you'll want to have at least one parent present for each child; after 3 years old, children usually behave better and have more fun if their own parents aren't present. When other parents are present at your party, despite your best intentions, you will find yourself catering to their needs as well as those of the children. Ultimately, this is very exhausting and seldom satisfying.

Remember that the more similar the ages of the guests, the more likely it is that the party will go smoothly.

- Let your child help with the guest list. You should offer choices or make suggestions, don't just ask an open ended question about who the child wants to invite. Sometimes there is a guest you know must be invited and you will have to be firm about such a decision, but give weight to your child's feelings about this rather than dismissing them lightly.

- Invite one guest for each year of your child's life, say some, or one for each year plus one, (for example, five children for a fourth birthday, six children for a fifth birthday, etc.).

- Or follow one professional party entertainer's rule: If you're courageous, if the birthday child is at least 4 years old, and if you have good help, 8 to 15 children may be the ideal number for the most fun.

- Parties for boys will need to move faster than those for girls. Generally speaking, boys' energy levels are higher and their attention spans shorter.

- Plan on including siblings unless they're likely to be very disruptive. An older child may be able to help with games and serving, and you may invite Grandma or get a sitter to help with a very young child. It's important to be sure the birthday child will not be upstaged, though.

Hired–or *Acquired*–Help

Everything will be much easier if you have help—a spouse, friend, relative, older sibling, or babysitter who will assist with games and activities as well as with serving and cleanup. Helpers can make the difference between a frantic-versus- smooth running party. While you cut the cake, your helper can be pouring drinks; while you monitor one game, your helper can be setting up for the next one. At first and second birthday parties, you'll probably have at least one parent for each child available for extra help, but after that you're on your own. Helpers can also be in charge of taking pictures, grilling hamburgers, providing face-painting, and helping children find the bathroom.

The best ratio is generally 2 adults to 8 children; but 2 adults are the minimum required to keep things running smoothly at any party. Here are some ideas for finding and working with party helpers:

• Spouses can be important helpmates in running a party smoothly. Discuss beforehand—in detail—how to share the party chores and entertainment.

• A good friend who is the parent of one of the party guests can be recruited (and the favor can be reciprocated later).

• Grandparents can be "organized" to assist, but only if that is their style. If they don't visit regularly or help out in your home, this is not the time to recruit them. Teens aged 14 to 16 make excellent helpers. They join in games more enthusiastically and less condescendingly than adults.

• Hire your child's regular sitter and be specific in what you will need help with. Don't pay regular hourly sitters' rates. Pay a flat fee that makes this worthwhile for both of you.

• Hire an older child or sibling and make this a real job with a real fee. Make sure he or she understands that cleanup is included in the job.

• Assign specific jobs to someone, whether yourself or your helper(s), so there is no confusion about who will be scooping ice cream or getting out the next activity.

Father Involvement

• Encourage (and a lot of encouragement may be needed!) Dad to help with every detail of party planning, from the guest list to the choice of games to the departure hour.

• Ask Dad to take charge of any decorations that can be set up the night before the party, such as hanging mobiles and streamers (no crepe paper streamers outdoors before the day of the party, though), clearing out and arranging the party room, or setting out the table and chairs.

• Consider scheduling the party for a time when Dad can participate fully or at least arrive home in time to greet the children, drive the guests home and/or help with the cleanup.

Birthday child's age: _____   Date: _____ Day of week: ___
Time: _____   Place: _____
Theme, if using one: _____   Entertainer, if having one: ____
Number of guests: _____   # of invitations needed: _____

Guest List

Names of Children	Address	Phone #	(Parent)	Reply

Adult Friends and Relatives:

Name	Address	Phone #	Reply

Helpers on Hand _____

Away-from-Home Party Possibilities:

Place/Address _____   Place/Address _____
Phone _____   Phone _____
Fee _____   Fee _____
Services included _____   Services included _____
Menu _____   Menu _____
Special considerations _____   Special considerations _____

Shopping List

Paper products, etc:
Invitations: _____
Stamps: _____
Plates: _____
Cups: _____
Tablecloth: _____
Place mats: _____
Candles: _____
Forks and spoons: _____
Napkins: _____
Balloons: _____
Decorations: _____
_____
_____
Favors: _____
_____
_____
Prizes: _____
_____
For a Treasure Hunt: _____
_____

Food:
Cake: _____
Order from: _____
_____
Phone: _____
Pickup date/time: _____
_____

If Homemade:
Ingredients _____
_____
_____
Frosting: _____
_____
Ice Cream: _____
Food favors: _____
_____
Drinks: _____
Food, if a meal: _____
_____
_____
_____

Materials for Activities & Crafts (*see Activity Planner List*):
_____
_____
_____
_____

And Don't Forget:
Camera/Camcorder/VCR: _____
Film/VHS tapes: _____
Audio cassettes/CDs/recorder: _____
Trashbags for cleanup: _____

What Kind of a Party Will It Be?

For small children home parties work best. They find it exciting to have a party with friends in familiar and comfortable surroundings. You don't have to have an elaborate party for it to be enjoyable. As you begin to plan, you will need to think about the ages of your guests, the space you have available, and the time of year and the weather to expect.

Before you send out invitations you'll need to decide whether the party will be indoors or outdoors so your guests will know what clothing will be appropriate. Your decision may be based on several considerations.

Planning for an Outdoor Party

An outdoor party is easier in many ways: easy cleanup, plenty of space, no rearranging of furniture or damage to the house. You need only cut the grass to ready the site.

But . . .

• Will the weather cooperate? There's no guarantee, of course. You'll have to have an alternate plan for moving indoors. Can you move the picnic table to the basement or garage and continue the picnic party there? You might be able to schedule a rain date, but children will be very disappointed if the party they've been looking forward to has to be postponed.

• Is your yard fenced so the party can be contained? If the fence is wooden, are there splinters or sharp points that can be dangerous for small children?

• Do you have a pool? Is it fenced so kids can't get to it unless you want them to, and will you have lots of helpers to watch them in case of an emergency?

• Are there poisonous plants in your yard that toddlers might try to eat? Some dangerous ones are oleander, rhododendron, azalea, bittersweet, nightshade, and lily of the valley (yes, those beautiful bell-shaped flowers are toxic!). Check also for mushrooms, as many types can be poisonous.

• Do you have a sprinkler system with pipes or spigots that kids might trip over?

We had a party for our 4-year-old in the gym of our local park. The kids brought trikes/bikes to ride while the parents rested between activities.
Karen Burkland, Sherman Oaks, CA

Planning for an Indoor Party

Don't wear yourself out cleaning the house or apartment. Straighten up for the adults a bit, but the children will never notice. Only your anxiety will show. And in a few hours you will have to be doing it all over again!

• Confine the party to 1 or 2 rooms for optimum efficiency: one for eating, the other for activities. Childproof both rooms according to the ages of the children and, if necessary, move some furniture out of the room or push it up against the wall.

• Be firm about the physical limits of the party. Keep bedroom doors closed if they're on the way to the bathroom. Remove keys from doors; remove anything in the party area that's even remotely precious. Your problems may be with "regulars"—the kids who are familiar with your house and feel at home there.

• Put away toys that won't be used for the party so they won't distract or tempt the guests.

• Tie streamers or place a safe, expandable gate (but not the accordion-style) across the entrance to any room that doesn't have a door.

• Be sure to designate a place for the children to put their coats and a place to stash presents safely until they're opened. If you don't have a good spot for the gifts, a decorated laundry basket is nice and portable.

Parties Away from Home

If you don't have your party at your home, you'll need to choose a restaurant or another spot for an outing. Partying outside your home has obvious advantages. You can come back to a clean house, a haven after an emotional and exhausting outing. But think carefully about it if you have children 4 or under. The danger in partying away from home with little children is that they will be difficult to manage and are likely to be overwhelmed by the excitement of an unfamiliar place. Parties away from home are more successful for children 5 years old and up. The novelty of these types of parties also can lose its appeal after repetitive birthday trips to the same location.

If you decide your house or apartment is not suitable for a party, or you're ready for a change, here are some ideas for places to consider taking the party:

- a child-oriented restaurant
- a zoo
- a video/pizza parlor
- a library at preschool story hour
- a movie or children's theater
- a hands-on museum
- a theme park
- a preschooler's gymnastic center
- a visit to the local fire department
- an airport or air show
- a train ride
- a local park for a picnic

For older children, consider:

- bowling
- miniature golf
- roller skating
- ice skating
- a gymnastics center
- an automatic pitching machine
- a sports center
- a pottery class
- renting equipment such as a moon-walk bounce house

Don't:

— have a swim party (or any other activity that requires lots of adult supervision and can be truly dangerous).

—visit the planetarium (or any other place that requires the children to sit still and be quiet for any length of time).

—have the party at Grandma's. She should enjoy—not work!

Fast-Food Chains

Many fast-food restaurants that specialize in hamburgers, pizza, and ice cream offer special rates and rooms for parties held in their establishment.

Be aware that two locations of the same franchise can be remarkably different. For sites that offer private party rooms and will make special arrangements talk to other parents and call more than one location of a franchise to obtain a description of the party area and their services.

Call ahead in plenty of time to make reservations in a private room, if they offer one, or plan to be there at a time when you can have a corner to yourself.

Order the same thing for everyone, or offer only two options. Offering more choices will just lead to confusion.

When you call the restaurant, be prepared to ask very specific questions:

• What *exactly* is offered in the way of food, table decorations, favors, and activities, and at what cost?

But Is It Worth It?

Before you sign up for any fast-food restaurant, consider these parents' experiences:

The worst party I can remember was one for 3-year-olds at a pizza place. The children were terrified of the people dressed in animal costumes and clung to their moms.

Karen Dockrey, Burke, VA

The worst party we experienced was at a hamburger chain restaurant. The noise and confusion were awful. The birthday child seemed to get lost in the shuffle. And all this was topped off by poor food. Yuck!

Judi Hoey, Morristown, NJ

My children have not enjoyed parties at hamburger fast-food places where they were expected to behave and sit still. Both of my children prefer parties in people's houses with not too many children. The best one was outside!

Harriet Landry, Belford, NJ

I didn't keep track of how many kids my 4-year-old social butterfly had invited to McDonald's. I had to pay for all fourteen!

Karen Miller, Long Lake, MN

Just to balance this account, it is necessary to report that half a class of Montessori preschoolers interviewed preferred a party at a hamburger fast-food chain over a home party!

- How long is the party expected to last?
- Are there suggested ages for guests attending the party?
- Is a minimum or maximum number of guests required?
- Does the birthday child get special recognition and attention?

Party Themes

Some parents find it easier to plan birthday parties if they start with a theme around which they can organize invitations, decorations, refreshments, and activities. Browsing through the party supplies at a card shop or department store will probably give you enough ideas for a dozen theme parties. Your child's favorite stories, interests, or songs can also spark your imagination. Or you can check with friends, relatives, and teachers for ideas.

Don't feel, however, that you must create a theme to build the party around. Remember, your party already has one theme: it's a birthday party.

Some traditional ideas for theme parties are described in Chapter 10. Most are for children 3 and up. Don't go overboard with decorations and elaborately structured activities. Small children won't (can't) appreciate your efforts, and they may be overwhelmed by too much organization and your need to attend to peripheral details.

Entertainers?

After you've considered the ages, interests, and attention spans of the children who will be at the party, you may decide that you want someone to come in and entertain them for a half-hour or so or run the party activities. Preschoolers have short attention spans, so a show should not be planned for more than 25 or 30 minutes. Consider entertainers who have been recommended by friends, relatives, or an agency. You can also check in the Yellow Pages or the newspaper classifieds, local parenting papers, and even your local children's hospital. For young children especially, don't let the entertainer be a surprise; it may prove to be terrifying rather than terrific. One mother attended a party that was going well until Superwoman suddenly (and unexpectedly) climbed over the backyard fence, scaring the 3-year-old guests.

Magicians can provide wonderful entertainment for kids, but only if the children are old enough to understand the concept of magic—probably at 5 or 6.

Hiring Considerations

Everybody's favorite, the clown, can satisfy even quite small children if it's understood that he or she will put on a very brief show for toddlers and be available to circulate and entertain during the rest of the party. Ask your potential clown entertainer how he or she handles small children who have never seen or been close to a clown before. Some put on their costume as part of the act, in order not to frighten small children.

• Be sure the entertainer is used to working with children and will be able to handle outbursts or lack of attention.

• Ask for names and phone numbers of satisfied customers, then call them for references. Does he or she have a video tape for you to see? Make sure you ask about their charges.

• Get all the details before you hire an entertainer. Some will provide favors, for example, and you need to know that ahead of time. How long is the performance? Does this person have different shows for different ages?

- Let the entertainer know about any potential problems that may arise with specific children, such as one who's handicapped or one who's afraid of animals, so he or she can adjust the show accordingly.

- Prepare the children for the type of entertainment they'll be seeing. Introduce your entertainer and tell the kids what kinds of things they'll be seeing and hearing.

You can check with the local high schools, colleges, and churches or your parks/recreation department to find aspiring young entertainers who should charge less than professionals and may do a wonderful job. You might find a teenager in your neighborhood who puts on fine puppet shows. Perhaps you can even convince Dad to get into a costume!

Video Entertainment

Home movie projectors have recently given way to VCRs. You can rent a VCR playback ($3 to $10 per day—credit card for security deposit) if you don't own one, along with the tapes to show on it. A feature movie is too long for most young children's attention span, especially for an entire group. Shorts or cartoons are good choices. Remember that most major libraries have good selections of videotapes at less expensive rental rates.

> **The worst party we've encountered had a viewing of *The Empire Strikes Back* on a VCR. It was mayhem!**
>
> *Myra Weaver, Hollywood, FL*

A Slumber Party?

Having 1 or 2 children sleep over can be a very special way to celebrate a birthday. The age and maturity of your child, as well as your child's friends, will be the significant factor in your decision. Perhaps your child's best friend is not yet ready to sleep away from home. This is not uncommon.

A Surprise Party?

Surprise parties are rarely successful for children under the age of 12. Remember half the fun for little children is the anticipation!

A Preschool/School Party

Most elementary and preschools celebrate a child's birthday and are open to a parent bringing treats for the class. Even children with summer birthdays usually get to celebrate their half-birthday during the school year. Teachers each have their own rules and guidelines which you will need to follow.

Store-bought treats may be required for health regulations. Bakery cupcakes that children can decorate with candies and icings are popular, as are packaged frozen fruit and ice cream bars.

Classroom parties are most common in preschool through third grade. Take cues from your child and check with the teacher for guidance. School parties are usually brief so keep everything simple. Restore room to pre-party condition before you leave.

> **Our elementary school principal reads the birthday child's name over the loud speaker. The child goes to the office and is given a pencil and a coupon for a birthday cookie.**
>
> *Jill Shellum, Richfield, MN*

Profit from Our Mistakes

The worst birthday parties I've given and attended were for children under 4. They're too young to appreciate being the honored one or being a guest. As hosts, they want to win all the games and keep all the prizes. As guests, they want to keep the presents for themselves. Parents tend to invite too many children for too many hours.

Karen Gromada, Cincinnati, OH

The very worst birthday party was the one I had for my 6-year-old (obviously my first child). We invited her entire first-grade class of 32. Pandemonium resulted, with all scheduled games played in half the time allotted, kids fighting all over the house, and screaming you wouldn't believe. My second child was allowed to invite only 6 kids to her sixth birthday party, and I think my third had 4.

Kathryn Ring, Scottsdale, AZ

I once made the mistake of inviting the mothers as well as the kids. I had a simple lunch planned for the children and an elaborate one for the mothers *(buffet-style)*. There was no way I could keep both groups happy.

Linda Phelps, Clarendon Hills, PA

The very worst birthday party was for a 4-year-old, attended by 2 children and 10 adult relatives. All I heard was, "Quiet down. Don't be so noisy." It wasn't even fun for me!

Kathy Hickok, Delray Beach, FL

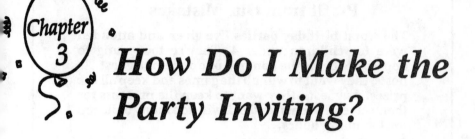

How Do I Make the Party Inviting?

Chapter 3

Sometimes you may feel that you must invite certain children, more than you had wanted to, because you must reciprocate. Not true! You've got to plan a party that will work for your child.

You can invite the guests by phone or by mail, or you and your child can hand-deliver special invitations. Just don't plan to have a child hand out invitations at school, nursery school, or Sunday school, or you'll also be inviting all sorts of trouble, ranging from the loss of all the cards to the hurt feelings of children who aren't invited. Send out invitations at least 10 days or 2 weeks before the party, if possible.

Invitations

Invitations are an important part of your party. They set the mood, tell what kind of party it will be, and help your child's anticipation get going. More often than not, we buy invitations (which the birthday child can help pick out), but you can also make them. Actually, this can be a fun project, especially if your child is old enough to help. Even the youngest child can put decorative stickers on invitation cards.

If your child's friends live in the neighborhood, you might let your child hand-deliver the invitations. If you have decided on a theme such as a circus party, the birthday child could dress up as a clown to deliver them.

If you choose to invite by phone, let your child extend the invitation to the guests if he or she wants to, but you will want to follow up with a call to the parent. Write down all the information before you start calling so you won't forget anything, and be very clear about the details.

Homemade Invitations

• Buy blank postcards and let your child decorate them. You may wish to save space by typing the party information.

• Use a recent photo of your child as a postcard, or, if you need all the space on the back for the information, slip the photo into an envelope.

• Cut birthday gift wrap or plain paper into clever shapes, a little smaller than the envelopes, and write all the information on the blank side. Good patterns for cutouts can be found in children's picture books or coloring books—you can trace them on to graph paper to enlarge easily if necessary.

• Decorate plain paper invitations with stickers, pictures cut from magazines, your child's drawings, or rubber stamp designs. Glue on sequins, buttons, or pieces of ribbon.

• Buy precut blank puzzles and write the information on them before you break them apart. Or make your own puzzles by writing on plain index cards before cutting them into several not-too-difficult pieces.

• Blow up a balloon, slip the invitation inside, and then let the air out. (It may be best to include a note in the envelopes telling invitees to blow up and pop the balloons.) Or blow up the balloon, write the information on it with a ballpoint pen or marker, then deflate the balloon, put it in an envelope and hand-deliver or mail.

• Cut out strips of paper dolls, hearts, or other shapes and write the invitations on them, one piece of information per shape.

• Photocopy a birth announcement or birth certificate for the "cover" of the invitation. Party details can go on the back.

• Mail the party invitation with glitter or confetti inside the envelope so that it spills out when the invitation is opened.

• Design your invitation to coordinate to the party theme if you are using one: a palette shape for an artist party; a plastic shovel for a beach party invitation; a wooden spoon for a cooking party; a dinosaur shape (traced around a dinosaur cookie cutter) for a prehistoric party; an invitation written on a paper napkin from the fast-food restaurant you selected as the party location. Use your imagination!

• Write a simple poem: "The time has come for birthday cake, It's my day for which we'll bake, A cake so glorious you will see, Please come over and share it with me," is an example.

• Use a computer to design your own invitation (many copy centers offer computer rental by the hour).

• Create a master invitation, then make a copy for each guest. The invitations may be copied on brightly colored paper; matching envelopes are usually available.

Specialized Invitations

Puzzled about where to get **blank puzzle notes** to write out your message? These blank puzzles come in white but you can always spray paint and decorate them first before writing out the party information. If you can't find them at your local card shop, you can order them by mail from:

> BITS AND PIECES
> 1 Puzzle Place
> B8016
> Stevens Point, WI 54481-7199
> 1-800-JIG-SAWS (544-7297)

With a computer you can create not only cards, but banners, name tags, place mats, place cards, or award certificates. Check your local computer software store. You'll find software featuring current popular cartoon and movie characters. Here are two to look for:

Print Power Pro   The Print Shop
Hi Tech Expressions   *Broderbund Software*

Or look for a CD ROM program such as:
The Print Shop Deluxe
CD ROM Ensemble

Special Hand-Delivered Invitations

• Cupcakes, with invitations folded and "cornered" into the frosting.

• Boxes of animal crackers with invitations tucked inside them.

• Decorated baskets, bags, or boxes containing party information written or typed on neatly folded pictures, cutouts, or paper flowers.

• Bags or boxes of popcorn which have been decorated with the invitation.

• A blown-up balloon with an invitation attached.

Information to Include

• *Whose party it is.* Be sure it's clear that it's a birthday party; nothing is worse than being the only one not bringing a gift because he or she didn't know it was a birthday party. It's also helpful to mention how old the birthday child will be—relatives especially may have a hard time keeping track.

• *Where the party will be.* If you think it's necessary or helpful, include a photocopied map or directions to your house.

• *The date and time of the party.* Remember, the ending time is as important as the beginning time. Don't forget to add that you'll be taking the children home, if that will be the case.

• *Special instructions,* such as, "Wear play clothes for an outdoor party," "Bring swimsuit," or "Bring high chair or infant seat or toddler's own bottle or cup."

• *What will be served:* lunch, supper, or just cake and ice cream.

• *Your request that parents accompany children,* if that's the case.

• *RSVP,* with your phone number and the date by which you need the answer. *Very important!!*

When the RSVPs Come In

• Ask if there are food allergies or other problems you should know about and prepare for.

• Also be prepared to give gift suggestions to those who ask.

• Tell parents which other children are invited so carpools can be arranged.

• If someone doesn't respond by the date requested, call them to be sure the invitation was received. You need to know who's coming, and so does your child.

No-Shows

Guests have been known to fail to turn up because of a communicable illness, broken bone, transportation problems, a last-minute conflict of schedules, and sometimes, just simple forgetfulness. Keep your sense of humor and a sense of perspective and you'll keep your friends, too.

Party Countdown Plan

2 Weeks Ahead: Discuss plans with your child if he or she is old enough to help make decisions. Check your camera, flash attachment, VCR, tape recorder, or any other equipment you intend to use to be sure it works. This will give you enough time to fix anything requiring repair. Send invitations.

1 Week Ahead: Check off RSVPs received and call any parents who have not responded. Invite other guests if many originally invited cannot come. Buy or make decorations. Order cake. Get prizes, favors, and any supplies you'll need for decorations and activities, such as paper, scissors, and glue.

3 Days Ahead: Buy groceries. Pick up any chairs, tables, or props you're borrowing. Check out records or tapes from the library and try them out. Order the cake if you forgot to, or buy any ingredients needed to bake one.

1 Day Ahead: Bake the cake or pick one up from the bakery (hide it!); prepare any food you can. Wait—don't blow up the balloons yet! Put together the favor bags.

5 Hours Ahead: Finish the food preparation. Prepare room or yard, set up decorations. Pick up helium balloons or blow up regular ones. Put prizes and activity supplies near the places where they'll be used. Set the table. Remember to allow adequate time to get yourself dressed before the party begins.

1 Hour Ahead: Help your child get dressed. Set up food and serving trays. Let your child help with as much as he or she can.

Let the Fun Begin!

Chapter 4

That First Birthday Party

Let's be honest: your child's first birthday party is really for you and the family. Your hands will guide tiny ones in opening the presents, you will blow out the candles, and you will accept the congratulations. The party will not be meaningful for your 1-year-old, and you won't hurt his or her feelings if you choose to make it a celebration for adults only—really a celebration of the anniversary of your becoming a parent.

A 1-year-old will experience the atmosphere of the occasion and delight in the attention, but the concept of a party is not within his or her grasp. The birthday child of this age has been known to be far more intrigued with the boxes and wrapping paper than with the gifts.

If you do decide on a party with other children or babies present, you may wish to do the inviting by phone, because you'll have a lot of information to convey. Make it perfectly clear that at least one parent must accompany every child, and get across the idea that older children are not invited, if that's the case. Plan on a very short party, unless you have plenty of room and equipment so the babies can go to bed while the adults enjoy themselves. Take your child's nap schedule into consideration. And childproof your play area carefully, remembering that it will probably contain both crawling and walking (staggering!) babies.

Guests

- Be clear that each parent is in charge of his or her own baby.

- Make it a BYO___ (*Bring Your Own___*) party, with the guests supplying their own *(highchairs, strollers, bottles, etc.)*.

- Be sure your child has had some exposure to other people, including other babies, before planning the party so their presence won't come as too much of a shock. If you're worried about your child's reaction, an adults-only party may be the way to go!

Refreshments

- Save the big birthday cake for the adults and let the babies have an unfrosted cupcake to minimize the mess.

- Or go ahead and frost the cupcakes. Faces smeared with frosting make for wonderful photos and happy memories.

- Serve ice cream to the babies in small cones for easier eating.

- Consider teething biscuits as appropriate treats (or wrapped, as party favors). Provide only chokeproof edibles.

- Place your child in a high chair at candle-blow-out-time so he or she doesn't accidentally fall forward into the lighted candle.

- Seat the children on small chairs or boxes around a low table if they won't be in high chairs. Expect that there'll be lots of getting up and going to Mommy or Daddy.

- Skip buying the cute paper tablecloth and napkins—they're likely to be torn and eaten.

- Set up a salad or sandwich bar for adults so they can eat at their convenience. Or be practical and offer the adults finger foods that can be enjoyed even while holding a baby on one arm.

Activities to consider? Walker races; crawl to the ball race; toy swap (ask each parent to bring one toy from home so the children can have the fun of a "new" toy to play with for the duration of the party). Entertain the little ones with blowing bubbles and/or finger play songs.

For the first birthday, the thing you should be most generous with is your camera (and film). Photos will furnish your child's only recollection of this first party. Take a picture of the front page of your daily newspaper. Be sure to take a photo of your new 1-year-old freshly dressed in the birthday outfit before the guests arrive. You might take a photo of the birthday child with each adult present; the pictures are wonderful for posterity—and make nice insertions into thank-you notes. Plant a tree in your yard and photograph your child next to it (and every year thereafter).

The Golden Birthday

This happens only once in a person's life. It is the birthday when the day of the month coincides with the chronological age. For example, if your birthday is on the fifteenth of the month, your fifteenth birthday will be your Golden Birthday.

Timing of Activities

The basic segments of a birthday party after the first year are:

1. Guest arrival and beginning activity

2. Events, activities, and/or entertainment

3. Refreshments

4. Opening presents, distributing favors, and farewells

Below are two loose schedules that may help you plan the timing of your party activities. Keep in mind that the time suggested for refreshments includes serving time; eating cake and ice cream usually takes only a few minutes.

A Party of 1 to 1½ Hours

1. *Arrival:* 10 minutes, with free play for those who come earliest. Set out a few toys suitable for the children's ages and have someone to supervise them and help them get acquainted or play cooperatively.

2. *Opening gifts*: 15-30 minutes, depending on the number of guests, and how old they are.

3. *Refreshments*: 10–20 minutes, for ice cream and cake, 20-30 minutes for a lunch or supper.

4. *Structured activities*: 10–30 minutes, singing, reading stories, games, crafts, etc., depending on the ages of the children.

5. *Goodbyes*: 10 minutes, as children are picked up or as you get them ready to be taken home. If they are being picked up, plan for free play while they wait. Don't start an exciting game that they'll be reluctant to leave.

A Party of 2 to 2¹/₂ Hours

1. *Arrival*: 15 minutes, with free play or a game or activity that newcomers can easily join as they arrive.

2. *Special activity*: 25–45 minutes, for a major crafts project or an entertainer.

3. *Refreshments*: 15–30 minutes, depending on what you will be serving your guests.

4. *A hunt*: 5–10 minutes, planned to take place either before or after refreshments, or included as one of the games.

5. *Games*: 30 minutes, for approximately 4 to 7 games, either alternating between quiet and active games, or having the quiet games at the end of game time to settle the children down for the next event.

6. *Presents and goodbyes*: 20–30 minutes. The parents who arrive early to pick up their children can watch the gift-opening.

Opening Activities

Do give some thought to this important part of your planning. Choose an activity that allows guests to join in as they arrive. Craft activities seem to work best; several are described on pages 86-94. The activity can be as simple as setting out crayons and pages torn from coloring books to making an edible necklace of licorice strings, or as ambitious as tracing the outline of the children's bodies on large sheets of kraft paper for them to color. Another idea that even the younger children will enjoy is to unroll a long sheet of paper from a roll (white shelf paper works well), set out lots of assorted colored markers and leave the children to create their original "birthday mural".

> **As the children arrive, they take a seat around a large sheet of white paper. Each child designs a section, and it can be cut up and sent home with each child. You can have a theme, but it's not necessary.**
>
> *Linda Merry, St. Louis Park, MN*

Setting the Stage for Party Manners

Naturally you'd like your birthday child to be a beautifully behaved, courteous host or hostess, more concerned about the guests' pleasure than about his or her own. Forget it! It won't happen for a good many years. Parties often bring out the worst in very young children—your own and the guests. Don't ruin the party for your child by prompting or scolding; this isn't the time.

Talk about the party beforehand, though. We are so used to party traditions that we often forget to tell a 2- or 3-year-old what to expect. It's a good idea to talk about the sequence of events and the rules you expect to be followed. You can try to get a few simple messages about good manners across to all but the youngest of children. Just don't expect any finesse.

• Encourage your child to disguise his or her "me first" behavior, at least to the extent of saying hello to the guests before grabbing the presents.

• Remind your child that he or she is expected to say hello and goodbye to each guest.

• Teach your child some nice things to say if he or she receives identical gifts. Try, "I wanted another one, anyway," or, "It's good to have two of these." If a present duplicates something the child already has, it's probably best to say nothing.

• Prepare your child ahead of time for the end of the party. Show by your example that we say goodbye at the door and say thank you for the present, even if we can't remember what it was. (See page 122 for some thank-you suggestions.)

It's reasonable for a young child's birthday to be one time when being "selfish" is okay. The birthday child should not be expected to share the gifts or to let others play with them.

Party Music

Music can be a great addition to any birthday party. Use it in the background or during games that call for it, such as Musical Chairs or Statues. You can often change the pace of a party by changing the type of music you select.

• Playing quiet background music while the children are eating can help maintain a quiet mood.

• Check out special "happy birthday" records or tapes from the library or look for them in record stores. Some that are available use Sesame Street, Winnie the Pooh, and Raggedy Ann and Andy themes.

• Try a sing-along with familiar songs, perhaps as an opening activity or at the end of the party. If you know someone who plays the guitar, the children will enjoy a "live" sing-along.

A Personalized Birthday Song

Order a personalized Happy Birthday audio *or* video cassette sung by "Captain Zoom." Your child's name will be sung eight times. To get a list of available names, send a self-addressed stamped envelope to:
> American Pro
> P.O. Box 2220
> Natick, MA 01760
> (508) 650-3805

Order a personalized audio birthday tape for $7.50 plus $1.50 postage (allow 2-3 weeks for delivery) for ANY name from:
> Cake & Candle Cassettes, Inc.
> P.O. Box 520309
> Winthrop, MA 02152-0006
> (617) 846-8831

Party Memories

Movies and videotapes are wonderful for recording all the action and excitement of a birthday party, but be sure to take some still pictures, too, for the family album. Many parents like to make up a separate album or scrapbook for each child's parties over the years, assembling the photos in the order in which they were taken. Consider including any of the following: a sample invitation, your child's place card, some birthday cards received, the menu, and a list of the games played.

Help a child of 4 or older start a party scrapbook. Use a three-ring notebook with both plain and lined paper and some heavy dividers with pockets. Ribbons, scraps of wrapping paper, an invitation, newspaper headlines from the big day, and snapshots can be pasted on the plain paper. Include an outline drawn of the birthday child's hand, the guest list, gifts received, the party menu. Other things you want remembered may be recorded on the lined paper. Mementos like birthday cards and small favors can be saved in the pockets. (Or you may want to use or copy the *Birthday Memory Record Sheets* on pages 152-153.)

Still Photos

• Consider getting an adult friend, a sitter, or spouse to take the pictures so you can devote yourself to the children. Yes, you can do it yourself, but you'll be spreading yourself pretty thin.

• Prepare the area you will be taking pictures by opening all the shades or curtains and turning on as many lights as possible. The more light you have the better quality of your images. (This also applies to video photography.)

• To take a group photo, tell the children you're going to count to three and take one "serious" pose. Next tell them they can be as "goofy" as they want to be while you count again; you'll probably get two photos worth saving! You can also try to photograph the children while they're playing an active game, or while they're dancing or singing.

• Use an instant camera, if you have one, for some of the photos; you'll know immediately if you've got the pictures you want. Try to be inconspicuous taking them if you are not prepared to have the kids get too engrossed in watching the film develop.

• Use a zoom lens to get close-in on children's expressions.

• Purchase a collage frame and add a birthday photo each year. You can personalize it with press-type for name and age. (If empty frames bother you, fill them with extra pictures from this year's party, and replace them next year.)

• Try for variety in your photos: if you're indoors, stand on a chair, stool or step and shoot downward. Outdoors, a picnic table will do. For an unusual picture, lie on the floor and have the children stand around you in a circle, looking down at you (don't forget to use your flash!). Spend time on your knees at the children's level for really good photos.

• Remember to take pictures of the birthday decorations, the cake, and the party table before the party begins, while they're all still in one piece!

• Take a snapshot of your child with each guest and use them later as thank-you notes.

Videotapes

- Borrow or rent a video camera for the occasion. Children are fascinated with both the instant replay of themselves and watching themselves on the VCR using previous videos.

- Check for batteries and fresh videotape BEFORE the party.

- Keep in mind that it's the party that's important, not the film you're making. It's easy to get carried away, but necessary that you don't! Make sure that the adult in charge of the camera understands that it is to be used sparingly, unobtrusively, and with a sensitivity to children, who may be intimidated.

- Remove a lamp shade if you need more light indoors.

- Make an annual event of taking party pictures. It's a wonderful way to chart children's growth from year to year.

- If you have old motion pictures of family events, they can be transferred onto video cassettes. They make for wonderful family entertainment.

- Never discourage girls or boys from wearing fancy party clothes. Children love to be photographed all dressed up, and fancy clothes often help to quell wild antics.

- Reserve an exclusive tape for birthday party footage for each of your children. You can give it to your child as a lasting memory of his or her childhood birthdays to take along with them when they reach adulthood and leave home.

- If you've hired an entertainer, be sure to tape the children's reactions as well as the performance. Ditto for gift opening. Secretly ask kids which present they brought (before gifts are opened) so you can quickly pan to the child who gave the gift.

• When photographing the opening of gifts, start with a close-up of the wrapped present. Zoom out as unwrapping begins. Focus on the child's reaction before going to the gift itself.

• Don't put the camera away when the party is officially over. Get some shots of the birthday child saying goodbye to guests, enjoying a gift in private or sharing a moment with a parent.

Let Them Eat Cake... and Other Yummies!

What is a party to little kids but cake and ice cream? You may be able to skip some of the other elements of the perfect party, but never the refreshments. You can't go wrong if you serve only ice cream and cake. If your party is for very young children, don't hesitate to serve the food soon after they arrive.

Limiting the amount of sugar at birthday parties is a personal decision. Most of us tend to throw strict nutritional guidelines out the window for this annual event. It's hard to know if sugar alone really contributes to hyperactivity at a children's birthday party because the party itself usually causes its own emotional high.

The Cake!!

For children the CAKE is the party. Whether helping to select it, making it, serving it, eating it, or just admiring it, for children the cake has a way of becoming the focal point of the whole wonderful birthday ritual.

Obviously, the easiest way to produce the most lavish, gorgeous birthday cake the guests have ever seen is to call the best bakery in town and order it, baked and decorated to your specifications. For children old enough to appreciate this luxury, it may be worth the expense. Kids under 10 will be satisfied with almost anything as long as it's sweet, covered with plenty of frosting, and blazing with candles. In fact, if the frosting and candles are impressive enough, the quality of the cake will not matter. A plain, commercially made or box cake mix variety with an icing chosen and applied by the birthday child can itself be a birthday highlight.

Tradition plays a large part in birthday celebrations, and one of the oldest traditions is that the birthday child is entitled to the first piece of cake, and to his or her choice of which piece. That preference is usually one with a candle or a frosting flower on it. Actually, all of the guests would probably prefer a piece with a decoration, and you might take this into consideration when you're decorating or ordering the cake. Make the decorations as large as possible to cover as much of the cake as possible. Or you might have a separate plate for decorations, and add one to each piece of cake after you cut it.

The song that accompanies every birthday party and the one without which no party is complete is, of course, "Happy Birthday To You." Traditionally, this is sung when the cake is carried in or after the candles are lit and before they're blown out.

HAPPY BIRTHDAY TO YOU
GG   A   G   C   B

HAPPY BIRTHDAY TO YOU
GG   A   G   D   C

HAPPY BIRTHDAY DEAR _____
GG   G   E   C   B   A

HAPPY BIRTHDAY TO YOU!
FF   E   C   D   C

(key of C)

Candle Power

Practice makes perfect. A 2-year-old will enjoy learning and singing "Happy Birthday" prior to the party. The other skill to practice is how to blow out candles. Use a straw to explain the technique if your child can't copy your mouth movements.

• Remember that lighted candles can be dangerous. Watch bows and ruffles, and be aware that a little girl's long hair can catch fire if she leans too close to the candles to blow them out.

• You can purchase a special 10 or 12-year birthday candle that can be used over and over as a special tradition.

• Serve the candlelit cake on a lazy Susan and give it a twirl for a fun effect before blowing out the candles.

• For a dramatic effect, turn off the lights to darken the room just before bringing in the lit birthday cake.

Cake Concoctions

Perhaps you have a favorite cake recipe (or one your mother made for you as a child). White, yellow, chocolate or angel food cakes are usually safe choices with children. Carrot cake with a cream cheese frosting and iced zucchini bread are more nutritious choices, but children who have never tasted any kind of cake but yellow, white, or chocolate may refuse to eat anything unfamiliar. It's usually best to stick with the tried-and-true for birthday cakes if you have no special dietary concerns. If you are making a cake from scratch that you haven't made before, do a practice run a week or so before the party. Nothing is more frustrating than having a cake not turn out to your satisfaction when you have all the other party details to attend to.

If you want to be a bit daring, consider one of these popular variations on the traditional cake:

• Make an ice cream cake by unwrapping a block of ice cream and covering it with lady fingers or other cookies. Return it to the freezer until ready to serve.

• Serve a platter of cupcakes with decorations and candles blazing. The advantages—pre-cut, easy-to-serve, all portions the same size—are obvious! Or arrange chocolate and vanilla frosted cupcakes to "spell out' the message with the first five cupcakes spelling H-A-P-P-Y, the next eight spelling B-I-R-T-H-D-A-Y and then as many as you need to spell out your child's name. Kids can choose their favorite flavor.

• Make a tiered cake using frosted cupcakes. Start with a circle of 7 cupcakes topped with M & Ms™, sprinkles, etc., then add a tier of 4, then 3, then 1. Add more candies, sprinkles and candles and you're done!

• Make a layered rainbow cake by dividing white cake batter into three parts, adding different food coloring to each part for a three-color cake. Spread batter into separate pans; bake according to directions. Frost generously between layers.

• To make a train cake, cut a sheet cake into serving-size rectangles. Frost and decorate each piece; arrange pieces on serving tray to resemble a train.

• Before cutting a sheet cake into an unusual shape (such as a dinosaur), freeze it. To prevent additional crumbling before frosting, brush edges lightly with some jam or preserves.

• Make a "ghostly" cake by baking your batter in a gingerbread-man cake pan and icing it with white frosting.

• Create a "party favor" cake as follows: score a sheet cake into 2-inch squares. Turn it upside down and scoop out some cake every 2 inches or so with a melon scoop. Plastic wrap a tiny toy and insert one in each hole. Turn the cake back over, frost and mark scored sections with a knife. When ready to serve, tell each child their piece will have a hidden, non-edible surprise!

• Stir a single raisin into the batter before baking the cake or cupcakes. Whoever gets the raisin wins a prize!

• Make cake cones by filling flat-bottomed ice cream cones half-full with the cake batter of your choice and place them on a cookie sheet or in a muffin tin. Bake according to directions for cupcakes. Or bake two at a time in your microwave for 45 seconds. Decorate them yourself or let the party guests do it.

Birthday Popcorn Cake

6 qts. popped popcorn
1 lb. gumdrops
1½ cups peanuts
1 large bag of
   marshmallows
½ cup salad oil
¼ cup margarine

Combine popcorn, gumdrops and peanuts in bowl. Melt the marshmallows, oil and margarine together over low heat and mix together well. Pour this over the popcorn mixture and mix well before placing in a greased angel food cake pan. Cool for 10 minutes and remove from pan. Decorate as desired.

• Or press your Rice Krispie® bar recipe (maybe a double batch) into a favorite cake form or into "cupcakes" in a muffin tin. Top with sprinkles, edible decorations or theme-related plastic toppers.

Frosting

Kids do judge a cake by its cover—the frosting! They don't care about nutrition, and seldom eat enough of any frosting to matter. You can make frosting from scratch or prepare it from a package or buy it ready-to-use in a can.

Freeze the cake or cupcakes before frosting. Frozen cake will be easier to work with and the frosting will harden faster on a frozen or slightly defrosted cake.

To make a simply wonderful raspberry frosting or filling for either a homemade or store-bought angel food cake: Dissolve one teaspoon unflavored gelatin in one tablespoon hot water. Stir in one cup of raspberry jam and chill. Whip one pint of whipping cream and fold into jam when it is partially set Spread between layers, on top and sides of cake. Add any additional decorations or fruit and chill frosted cake before cutting.

Cake Connoisseurs

If unusual cake decorating lures you, you can be aided and abetted in your endeavors by using the books, molds, and products of Wilton Enterprises. Look for their books titled **Cake Decorating Yearbook** and **Cake Decorating...Easy as 1,2,3** or mail order from:

Wilton Enterprises
2240 W. 75th Street
Woodridge, IL 60517
1-800-794-5866
in Illinois call (708) 963-7100 ext. 320.

The Guest-Decorated Cake

If the party guests are at least 4 years old, and if there aren't too many of them, you may wish to let them help the birthday child decorate the cake. Buy or make a plain sheet cake and frost it with white icing. Then supply several tubes of different colored frosting for the guests. Write decorating ideas on pieces of paper ("*Write Happy Birthday*," "*Write Mary's name*," "*Make a border around the cake*," "*Add flowers*" etc.) and let each child make one addition to the cake. If you decide only one child at a time should work on the cake, let the others work simultaneously at decorating a paper tablecloth or place mats with crayons or markers

Another do-it-yourself delight is decorating birthday cupcakes. The project could be set out as an early activity or could be done just before eating them. Give the children wooden popsicle sticks for easy frosting spreaders. Divide prepared frosting among small bowls. Add a few drops of different food coloring to each bowl, along with flavorings like peppermint, lemon, or orange.

Then provide a variety of fun toppings like sugar sprinkles, animal crackers, gumdrops, carob or chocolate chips, M&Ms™, red hots, chopped peanuts, etc. and let the kids go to it!

Easy Frosting and Decorating Tidbits

• For a quick and easy frosting, sprinkle a cake or cupcakes still hot from the oven with chocolate chips. As the chips melt and soften, spread with a flat knife or spatula. Let cool before eating.

• Before frosting, slide pieces of waxed paper under the cake on all sides. When the cake is frosted, pull the papers out, and there'll be no drips or splatters on your serving plate.

• Use big gumdrops, marshmallows, or Lifesaver® candies as candle holders on the cake.

• Set a small glass filled with flowers—real or artificial—in the center of a tube cake.

• Decorate the top of the cake or cupcakes with miniature plastic figures that complement your party's theme.

• Use your child's favorite color to frost the cake even if you think it looks a bit outrageous.

• Create a balloon bouquet design on the frosted cake by using licorice strings and pastel colored mint wafers.

• To make a "gift-wrap" cake, decorate a frosted rectangular or square cake using red string licorice arranged on the cake to resemble a tied package. Make a bow of red licorice, cut-up fruit roll/leather or real ribbon to complete the gift wrap look.

• Use cookie cutters to imprint patterns in frosting and then outline the designs with tube frosting.

• Avoid frosting altogether by chilling cupcakes first, then dipping tops (now sticky) into sprinkles, decors, etc.

• Create "hot air balloon" cupcakes by attaching a blown-up balloon to a straw and inserting the straw into the center of a frosted cupcake. Next tie narrow ribbons from the bottom of the cupcake to the top of the balloon and secure them with tape.

• Decorate a round layer cake as a clock: frost the cake with chocolate frosting, then use tubes of white icing to draw a clock face with both hands pointing to the number of your child's age.

Ice Cream Serving Suggestions

Offer only one kind of ice cream; vanilla is probably your best bet. If you feel you must satisfy everyone, buy Neapolitan ice cream, (vanilla, chocolate, and strawberry packed in layers). Little kids don't eat the exotic. Actually, vanilla Dixie® Cups—wooden spoons and all—can be the most fun.

Homemade ice cream can be exciting for children over the age of 4, but only if you already have the equipment and have made it before. Timing is important; be sure to start freezing the ice cream before the party starts to ensure it is ready to eat before the guests leave.

• Consider serving ice cream in cones for easier handling. Or make ice cream clowns, with the cone mounted like hats on the scoop of ice cream and faces made out of various candies placed into the ice cream.

• Put a miniature marshmallow or two in the bottom of a pointed cone, or put a large marshmallow or a small cookie in a flat-bottomed cone to keep ice cream from leaking and to make a surprise treat at the end. For a nutritious alternative use a slice or two of banana.

• Scoop the ice cream into paper cups or cupcake papers and keep them in the freezer until you have cut and served the cake. Variation: roll the scoops in bits of colored candies or chocolate "jimmies" before freezing.

• Put a candle in each child's scoop of ice cream or cupcake so everyone gets to blow one candle out. (Be sure the birthday child blows his or hers out first!)

Planning the Other Refreshments

Are you going to serve a meal? It's not necessary, but it will keep children seated and occupied for longer than it takes to eat just ice cream and cake. If you are on a limited budget, don't serve a meal; cake and ice cream are all that's really needed.

As you plan try to keep in mind that the refreshments will be eaten—or not eaten—by children, perhaps finicky ones at that! If you decide to extend yourself and serve lunch or supper (best reserved for kids at least 4 or over), remember that this is not the time to try out the new quiche recipe or make tacos. Avoid messy foods like spaghetti or anything in gravy or sauce. An exception is Kraft's Macaroni and Cheese, an all-time favorite.

Choose foods that can be prepared ahead of time; avoid any that require last-minute preparation.

Serving snacks during games or activities will distract the kids, and you'll probably have lots of extra mess to clean up. Save all food to be eaten at the table.

Another good idea: set up a snack stand and give each guest play money to buy treats.

Remember the cardinal rule: *Keep it simple!*

Menu Ideas

Stick to the foods children like and can handle easily, even if the meal doesn't seem very festive to you: hot dogs (for older children only, due to choking hazard), hamburgers, pizza, peanut butter and jelly sandwiches, cheese cubes, vegetable sticks with a dip, and fruit are all fine. The fewer pieces of silverware you need on the table, the easier your lunch or supper will be for the kids—and therefore for you.

Sandwiches Slightly Different

• Make up a platter of small peanut butter and jelly sandwiches cut into triangles. (No crusts, please—after all, this is a party!)

• Cut sandwich bread with cookie cutters to make special shaped sandwiches (hearts, bunnies, etc.).

• Spread peanut butter on equal numbers of bread circles and triangles. Then make clown faces by arranging a triangle hat next to each circle face. Decorate the faces with jam, raisins, maraschino cherries, and coconut.

• Or spread peanut butter with honey and banana slices on hot dog buns.

• Make hero sandwiches with cold meats, egg or tuna salad, cheese—whatever you like. Poke holes in the crust and insert birthday candles. Serve tomato slices, lettuce, mayonnaise, pickles, and other additions on the side.

• Serve open-faced grilled cheese sandwiches on bagel halves or on bread cut into shapes with cookie cutters.

• Make miniature easy-to-handle pizzas on English muffin halves. Ready-to-bake individual pizzas are now readily available in the freezer case of most grocery stores as well.

• Serve miniature hamburgers on tiny cocktail buns. Or shape small hamburgers, place them between flattened-out refrigerator biscuits, crimp the edges together and bake according to package directions (about 20 minutes). For added zest, add a dollop of ketchup or barbecue sauce before sealing.

• To make pigs-in-a-blanket, wrap weiners in strips of refrigerated crescent roll dough, patted out flat. Bake at 400 degrees or roast over coals on the outdoor barbecue. If older kids will be roasting their own, let them make "shields" against the heat by poking the ends of the roasting sticks through foil pie plates before sticking on the wrapped weiners.

• Serve tuna or egg salad in ice cream cones for easy eating.

• Stuff celery sticks with peanut butter, cream cheese, American cheese spread, or tuna salad.

A super treat for kids to make for themselves is peanut butter roll-ups. Flatten one slice of bread with a rolling pin. Spread with peanut butter (add jelly, wheat germ, peanuts, anything you like). Roll like a jelly roll and cut off half-inch slices. Pop into mouth and smack lips.

M. Van Dan, Hebron, IL

Other Lunch and Supper Ideas

• Make whole meal kabobs on wooden popsicle sticks, using cubes of cheese, cold meat, melon balls, pineapple chunks, cherry tomatoes, pieces of green pepper, or any other fruits or vegetables you think the kids might eat.

• Make a "Happy Birthday Salad" by hollowing out the inside of a watermelon and filling it with cut-up fruit. Replace the top of the melon and insert candles into holes in the top's rind.

• Put a small serving of cottage cheese on a bed of shredded lettuce for each child. Decorate the cheese as a face with carrot or celery pieces ears, a peach slice smile, an olive nose, raisin eyes and matchstick-thin celery slice whiskers.

• Oven-fry small chicken drumsticks or wings, or buy cooked frozen chicken pieces and heat them up, and serve an assortment of dips for them—sweet and sour sauce, barbecue sauce, or plain ketchup.

• Give children individual bags of chips to avoid conflict.

Time to Eat ...

• Always seat the children and *bring the food to them!* You can set an attractive, convenient buffet table in a few years when the kids are old enough to serve themselves and carry loaded plates without inevitable accidents.

• Try to have the correct size table and chairs for little people.

And to Drink

• Don't serve beverages that stain (like grape juice).

• Offer juicebox cartons with straws inserted into carton-top holes. They are favorites, almost spill-proof, and save you the trouble of cups or glasses. Try apple or other fruit juices instead of less nutritious drinks. Plastic box holders are helpful for little ones who may squeeze the box and use it as a toy.

• Or buy and serve drinks in plain sip-top bottles decorated with party-theme stickers, kid's names or cut-out shapes from self-stick adhesive. These become take-home favors, too.

• Attach a brightly colored pipe cleaner (with a pom-pom added to one end) around a drinking straw to become a drinking wiggle worm, making any drink something special.

• Offer "rainbow" milk by adding food colorings to several pitchers of milk. A drop of vanilla adds a delightful taste.

• A small amount of cranberry juice mixed with lemonade makes pink lemonade—pretty and delicious!

• Mix sherbet and ginger ale for a punch that fizzes.

• Don't pour the drinks ahead of time at the table. Make sure each child is settled in a chair before filling the cups (only one-third or half full) to avoid major spills. Or you can fill them in another room and serve from a tray after everyone is seated.

For my son's 4th birthday we filled his red wagon, decorated with balloons on the handle, with ice and drinks. His cleaned-up dump trucks held chips and crackers. We pulled the wagon outside and the kids helped themselves. Easy cleanup!

Peggy Vann, Sonora, CA

Other Nuts and Bolts

• Don't serve nuts or hard candies to children 3 and under who could choke on them. (Beware, too, of hot dogs, as they are a leading cause of choking in young children. Serve only if cut into long, narrow strips as though they were carrot strips.)

• For children over 3, use a mixture of shelled peanuts, raisins, and M&M™ chocolate candies to fill nut cups if you feel they're necessary. Or use flat-bottom ice cream cones to hold little snacks at each child's table setting.

• Hand out wrapped popcorn balls or pretzels tied with a bright ribbon to take home as favors.

• Dried fruit rolls are popular additions to the table or favor bag. Form into a cone or cut into fun shapes. Tying a ribbon around packaged ones also makes them special for a party.

• To make Finger Jell-O®: dissolve two envelopes of unflavored gelatin in one cup of cold water and add one 6-ounce package of flavored gelatin to a cup of boiling water. Combine and add ½ cup of cold water. Chill in a lightly greased pan until solid. Use cookie cutters to make fancy shapes which complement your theme if you feel really creative.

• Use paper and plastic whenever possible. Although this may not be correct environmental advice, birthday parties happen just once a year and the disposable products will save you lots of cleanup time and worry about breakage.

• Wrap up all the empty paper plates and cups and the garbage in your paper tablecloth to throw away. Or have several large, heavy-duty plastic trash bags handy.

Forewarned Is Forearmed

• Expect small children to eat very little. It won't be because your refreshments aren't delicious but because the children will be too excited to bother with food. Make portions small; you can always serve seconds.

• Plan something for the fast eaters to do when they've finished. It's too much to expect kids to sit patiently (or quietly) at the table waiting for dawdlers.

• Consider reading stories or poems to the children while they eat; it may keep everyone content.

Even if you watch your child's diet throughout the year, taking care that no junk food ever passes his lips, this is the one day you ought to relax your restrictions. Console yourself that those sugary treats are an indulgence only once a year. I've had very bad luck with carrot sticks, sunflower seeds, and my nutritious, no-sugar munchies at kids' parties. The guests protested loudly, and the birthday child was very disappointed.

Mary McNamara, Wayzata, MN

Special Menus

If your child suffers from diabetes, lactose intolerance, or food allergies, or is on a special diet for hyperactivity/ADD or any other problem, you'll undoubtedly plan the party refreshments around his or her requirements. If the parent of a guest who has such problems offers to send along suitable food, accept gratefully. You can offer non-diet foods to the other children if you wish, but be prepared to watch carefully to make certain that the restricted child eats only what's allowed on his or her food plan.

Ice Cream Substitutes

Several milk and butterfat-free "ice creams" are now available. Check your local supermarket or ice cream store for them. The substitutes look like ice cream, taste like ice cream, and chances are good that only you will know the real thing. Other alternatives are fruit ices, sorbets, or Italian ices. They're colorful and tasty enough to appeal to kids. Be aware that most sherbet you buy in stores does contain milk.

Watermelon Sorbet

6 cups ripe watermelon, cut up and seeded
1 cup sugar
juice of ½ lemon

Blend watermelon with sugar in blender or food processor. Add lemon juice and stir well. Spoon mixture into an ice cube tray and freeze for 1½ hours. Remove and beat until smooth; return to freezer for several hours or overnight. Serve in small bowls and decorate with water- melon balls, if desired. Serves 4 to 6.

Milk-Free Ice Cream

1 (8 oz.) container Richwhip® topping (or any nondairy equivalent frozen whipped topping)
¼ cup sugar, or equivalent artificial sweetener
1 teaspoon vanilla
optional: 1 mashed banana, 1 cup berries or other fruit

Whip the topping as you would heavy cream. When thickened, add sugar, vanilla, and fruit (pureed or whole). Freeze for ½ hour. Remove and beat for one minute. Pour into a storage container, cover, and freeze. Natural it is not (read the ingredients listed on the topping carton), but milk-free and delicious it is! This mixture, if pureed well, can be used in an ice cream maker. Serves 4.

Banana/Carob Milk-Free Ice Cream

6 ripe bananas
3 tablespoons honey or sugar
¹/₃ cup oil
2 tablespoons carob powder
4 tablespoons powdered
   soy milk
¹/₂ cup water

Blend all ingredients and freeze.
Serves 6 to 8.

Birthday Cake Alternatives

If you haven't checked out your guests for possible allergies, you can use the following recipe (known to some as Crazy Cake) for an easy, good-tasting cake that contains no milk or eggs:

Diplomatic Cake (Milk-Free and Egg-Free)

1 cup sugar
1¹/₂ cups flour
3 tablespoons cocoa/ carob
   powder
1¹/₂ teaspoons baking soda
5 tablespoons salad oil
1 tablespoon vinegar
1 teaspoon vanilla
1 cup cold water

Combine dry ingredients, then pour in oil, vinegar, vanilla, and water, mixing well. Bake in 8"x8" pan at 350 degrees for 35-40 minutes. Frost or add icing after cake is cooled. Serves 6 to 8.

The Gluten-Free Birthday Cake

Buy a loaf of heavy rice bread, which looks like pound cake. Make a butter frosting with hot water, butter, margarine, or soybean margarine and powdered or confectioners' sugar. For coloring, use hot cranberry juice or grape juice. Because the bread is quite dry, lots of frosting is needed.

Other Treats

• Frozen bananas on a stick covered with honey or peanut butter and dipped in crushed nuts or seeds.

• Carob chips, dried banana chips, popcorn (for older kids).

• Parfaits layered with yogurt, berries, peanut butter, jams, chopped nuts and/or granola.

• Mini rice cakes topped with peanut butter.

• Fruit salads.

• Cantaloupe boats: Construct a sailboat by putting cheese slices *(sails)* on pretzel sticks or wooden sticks *(masts)* on a small wedge of cantaloupe. Fill the cantaloupe with grapes, and insert the sticks into the cantaloupe among the grapes.

My 2-year-old, who is very sensitive to gluten and most fresh fruits and vegetables, has been to two parties. For the first, I brought a loaf of banana rice bread with pink frosting. As it turned out, she ate potato chips the whole time—the cake situation didn't bother her. For the second party, I made a Jell-O® mold and frosted it with colored whipped cream. The mold was a success, but my daughter was more impressed by a few tastes of the white frosting on the gluten cake. In both cases, I was more upset than she was.

Karen Haynes, Albuquerque, NM

Creating the Party Magic: Decorations, Favors, and Prizes

Decorating is the magic you use that transforms your home and separates your child's day from all the rest of the days of the year to say, *"You're special!"*

You don't have to spend a lot of money to create a party mood. Yes, stores offer wonderful party decorations, but indulge in them only if your budget allows. Inexpensive or homemade decorations can be just as festive. Whether you buy or make them, let your child help as much as possible.

Decorative Materials

• Crepe paper for streamers

• Inexpensive posters

• A collection of stuffed animals and dolls

• Buy or make your own confetti. It's a great way to keep a child busy—with a hole puncher, colored paper, leftover gift wrap, old mail order catalogs, even aluminum foil. Confetti dresses up any table for children over the age of 3 who are no longer tempted to put it in their mouths. (And it vacuums up easily.)

Balloons by Mail

Buy 10 personalized *Happy Birthday* balloons for your birthday boy or girl. Specify "stem down" if you're using helium or "stem up" if you're just blowing them up. Print your child's name clearly, and send your order with $3.98 plus $1.95 for postage & handling (*item #RP 121-24*) to:

Miles Kimball
41 West 8th Avenue
Oshkosh, WI 54906

If you've wanted to learn how to make balloon animals as part of party entertainment or for decorations, send for any one of the following books by Aaron Hsu-Flanders: *Balloon Animals*, $15.95 and *More Balloon Animals*, $15.95. Each book comes with balloons and a pump. For phone orders with credit card, AmEx/MC/Visa/Discover, call customer service at 847-679-5500 or 800-323-4900. When ordering by mail, add $5.00 per title to cover postage & handling and send to:

NTC/Contemporary Books
4255 W Touhy Ave.
Lincolnwood, IL 60646.

For a do-it-yourself "Happy Helium Balloon Kit" (Twenty 3" balloons and enough helium in an aerosol-type can to inflate them), send $15.95 plus $4.95 for postage & handling (*item #71289*) to:

Edmund's Scientific
101 E. Gloucester Pike
Barrington, NJ 08007-1380
(609) 573-6250

Balloons

Balloons—lots of them—are musts for children's birthday parties, and fortunately, they're not necessarily expensive. Use dozens of them in all sizes, shapes, and colors, and look for some that have your child's name printed on them.

• Get out the old bicycle pump to make blowing up eaiser. Or pick up an inexpensive push pump at the variety store (usually stocked next to the balloons). Remember to stretch balloons first to make them easier to inflate.

• Don't buy helium balloons until party day. Some can lose their "holding" power in a day.

Warning

Swallowed or inhaled balloons or pieces of balloons present a serious suffocation threat. Be sure that children play with only inflated and intact balloons. And always immediately dispose of any ballons that break.

- Expect some balloons to pop, so buy them in quantity instead of in small packages. Do be careful to keep small pieces of popped balloons away from children under 3 who might put them in their mouths and choke.

- To simplify cleanup, let the kids take balloons home as favors.

Table Decorations

Remember that the less crowded the table the better. A too-large centerpiece and a lot of small items scattered about will produce spills in direct proportion to the inexperience and age of the party guests. As a safeguard against bowls tipping over and spilling their contents, you can attach them to the table with double-stick tape.

Centerpieces

- Attach a bunch of helium-filled balloons to the center of the table, adjusting them to float high enough so children can see across the table. Metal washers from the hardware store tied to the string of a floating balloon will anchor it to the table, if you want to have a balloon at each place setting. You can also buy anchors in party shops. Or you can tie or tape a balloon or two to the back of each chair.

- Use the birthday cake as the centerpiece. Setting it on a pedestal (even a sturdy box covered with foil or gift paper) will add to its magic. Its beauty will be appreciated more if it's seen for longer than the few minutes before the candles are blown out and the cake is cut. Remove the cake to light the candles, and bring it back for the "Happy Birthday" song. If the cake is within reach of the guests, expect fingerprints and taste marks.

• Set a big, pretty basket on the table and fill it with small balloons, popcorn balls or other treats wrapped in plastic wrap and tied with bright ribbons or yarn, small house plants, tiny stuffed animals, or anything pertaining to the party theme that could go home with the guests as favors.

• Streamers attached from the light fixture over the table to the corners of the room make a festive canopy. A mobile or a bunch of balloons looks great hung from the center of the fixture.

Paper Party Products by Mail

No time for shopping or can't find a convenient party store with a good selection of goods and favors? The following companies offer a variety of party items by mail. Just looking through their catalogs will give you ideas.

Paradise Products
Box 568, El Cerrito, CA 94530
(510) 524-8300 *$2 for catalog*

Birthday Express
11220 120th Ave. NE
Kirkland, WA 98033
(206) 250-1006

Stumps
One Party Place, PO Box 305
South Whitley, IN 46787
1-800-22-PARTY (72789) *Free Catalog*

Table Toppings

- Buy a plain white paper tablecloth that can be decorated in advance by the birthday child or by the guests as they arrive. Or cover the table with plain, heavy paper and let them scribble with crayons or markers while they wait to be served.

- Be sure whatever party tablecloth you use has a short drop that will not rest on the laps or knees of the children.

- Use sheets of the newspaper's colored comic section taped together as a colorful and inexpensive decorative table cover.

- Turn a child's colorful bed sheet into a festive tablecloth for use indoors or outside.

- Use a plain white tablecloth on which preschoolers can write their names. Later, stitch over the names and use the cloth year after year, adding new names and repeating old ones.

- Design your own place mat and make photocopies—let your imagination run wild! You could start with a picture of your child and let him or her embellish it. Or you could copy it on colored paper, let your child add to it with markers or crayons, and then cover the mats with clear contact paper.

- Supply colored construction paper for place mats and an assortment of washable markers or crayons for the children to decorate them with. The color may bleed onto the tablecloth if the paper gets wet, but it should wash out with no problem.

- Or buy solid-color vinyl placemats that children 5 and over can decorate with permanent markers or stickers and then take home as party favors. (Be sure your table is protected if you use permanent markers.) Or offer crayons and washable markers if you want to restore the place mats back to their original color.

• Use colorful napkins to perk up the party table if you're using plain white paper plates.

• A blanket can substitute as a protective table pad if you are worried about water damage to your dining room table.

Party Hats

Party hats, either homemade or store-bought, are a birthday party tradition that children have come to expect. In addition, they make for terrific party photos.

Hats may stay on small heads for a long time or a very short time. Children's ages, their comfort and sophistication each play a part. Most hats are loved at party time and as a take-home favor.

Do-It-Yourself Ideas

• Roll an 8" x 12" piece of colored construction paper into the shape of a cone, tape or staple closed. Decorate as you choose.

• Cut a piece of colored construction paper in half lengthwise in a zigzag pattern. Tape the ends together to form a headband that can be decorated as a crown.

• A simple fun party hat can be made of a decorated strip of sturdy colored paper to which you've attached small balloons or anything else that you like.

• Buy simple party hats and let the children decorate them with feathers, glitter, bows, fake flowers and such.

• Make ties to go under the chin using party ribbon, string, or long, substantial rubberbands that can be cut and knotted after threading them through the two side-holes in the hat.

Place Cards

Use place cards even if the children are too young to read them. Everybody will want to sit by the birthday child, and place cards lend an air of authority that will avoid trouble.

Consider making name tags for each guest, too. Wearing name tags make children feel important and may be helpful to you, too, when you forget a child's name.

• Tie helium balloons with names written on them to the backs of the children's chairs.

• Write names on cutouts of gingerbread boys, paper dolls, animals, etc. and set the cutouts on each plate at the table.

• Make paper cones of half-circles cut out of heavy brown paper and taped or stapled together. Decorate the cones with markers and stand them, straight side down, with a lollipop stuck in the center of each.

Table Settings as Place Cards

• Write the children's names with permanent markers on paper cups or, better, on hard plastic cups which will be less apt to tip.

• Write names on cutout paper shapes, punch a hole at the top and bottom and weave a drinking straw through the holes. Stick the straws into drinking cups or cupcakes.

• Use a paper tablecloth or an old white sheet and write the children's names on it at their places. Let the kids decorate the space around their names with crayons. Place brown paper on top of the names and drawings and iron gently (be sure there's adequate padding on the table under the cloth) until the crayon wax melts and lifts, leaving just the color on the cloth.

- Use a plain color paper plate and write the child's name in a circle around the border.

Food as Place Cards

- Make a place card necklace from sugar cookies (slice-and-bake refrigerator cookies will do nicely) or plain rectangular biscuit cookies. Cut into shapes, if you like, and make a hole at the top of each cookie before baking. Write each child's name on a cookie with frosting and thread string through the hole.

- Or make cookie puzzles: bake fairly large cookies; score lines for the pieces while they're warm, and break at divisions when they are cool. Fit them back together and write a child's name on each cookie with frosting from a tube .

- Or write the children's names on cookies with squeeze-bottle honey, then sprinkle with colored sugar (this can get messy!).

- Turn sugar ice cream cones upside down and write names on them with frosting. Use the cones later for serving ice cream.

Favors as Place Cards

- Put small toys or candies in plastic sandwich bags, then into empty cardboard toilet tissue cores you've saved for just such an occasion. Wrap the cores in party paper, comic strip paper, etc. and twist and tie up at the ends. Write the children's names with markers on the outside of the package .

- Write the children's names on the outsides of small paper bags (lunch bags are good), fill bags with candy and favors for each child. Fold over the tops and staple, tie up with ribbon or tape shut. Presto, party bags, ready-to-go!

• Make or buy party hats and write the kids' names on them.

• Serve each child's food on a clean new Frisbee® that has his or her name written around the outside edge. Use paper plates as liners to save yourself the trouble of cleaning the Frisbees® before they go home with the kids.

Place Cards to Use in Games or Activities

• Embroider or mark the children's names on beanbags which can then be used for a tossing game.

• Use a permanent marker to write the names on sandbox pails and shovels if there will be sandbox play at the party—then let the children take them home as favors.

• Write names on small clay pots that contain plastic bags of soil and some flower seeds. The children can plant seeds as a party activity or they can take them home to plant and watch grow.

Decorating Indoors

You need not decorate more of the house than the play area and the room where the food will be served. Decorating the front door, however, is a fun way to announce a party inside.

• If you rub blown-up balloons against your clothes to create static electricity, they should stick to walls and windows (or to your hair!) for from 12 to 24 hours.

• Tie crepe paper streamers or place a decorated, expandable gate across the entrance to any room that doesn't have a door.

• Attach streamers to your walls and ceiling with dabs of white toothpaste—it holds them quite well and will wash off easily.

• Or try attaching streamers or inexpensive posters to painted walls with small dabs of rubber cement. When it's time to take the posters down, the cement will roll up and rub off easily.

• Design and make your own paper mobiles by attaching cutouts to streamers at different lengths.

• Make mobiles of coat hangers hung with small dolls, cars, or other toys. Remember to hang them at all different lengths.

• Let preschoolers make streamers of colored paper chains they put together themselves from paper strips and glue.

• Draw theme art on posterboard for each child to color at the beginning of the party. Hang completed posters up around the room to decorate, then send them home asparty favors.

• Dress up your collection of stuffed animals or dolls with party hats and streamers and arrange them to decorate the room.

• Save decorations if they can be used again for another party.

Decorating Outdoors

• Tie some balloons to the front door or mailbox to announce the festivities and also to help guests find the house.

• Stretch a birthday banner across the front of the house or above the front door. It can be made from a roll of drawing or shelf paper or an old sheet, or can be purchased in a gift store.

• Make a path from the front door to the party area, with arrows pointing the way to the "Fairy Castle," the "Dragon's Lair," or "Raggedy Ann and Andy's House." For added anticipation, make footprints from construction paper for the kids to follow.

- String crepe paper streamers between bushes and trees to confine activities to appropriate areas.

- Or wrap two different color streamers around tree trunks to resemble candy canes.

- Hang thin ribbons of various colors from the lower branches of trees for a delicate, festive effect.

- Tie lots of multicolored balloons in bunches to trees and shrubs—the more, the better!

- Fasten bright posters to trees in the yard.

Party Favors

Favors are definitely called for, at every age. Just be sure they're alike in size, color, and appeal, to avoid conflict. Let your child help you choose and make the favors. The "party bags" (a.k.a. loot bags or goody bags) have become an accepted part of birthdays, it seems, so you may want to put together identical bags for each guest. Favors are fun when coordinated with your theme, making them even better souvenirs of your party.

Do not think kids won't like homemade favors—they appreciate any and all take-home items. And don't let fancy favors turn into a competitive item for you among your own peers.

Remember, when it comes to prizes, gifts, and possessions in general, preschoolers are self-centered, not selfish—there is a difference. *It is natural not to want to share at that age.* Selfishness involves understanding and rejecting the perspective of someone else. That's not the case with small children. They want to keep something to themselves because they do not fully understand the wishes or needs of others. And a birthday party is definitely not the place to try to teach children how to share!

Favors and Party Bags

• Avoid blowers. More often than not, children tend simply to blow them in each other's faces.

• Don't forget to provide identical party favors and a party bag for the birthday child as well as for the guests.

• Use favorite or theme-related containers as party "bags." These can be beach pails, mugs, paper hats, cosmetic bags, fanny packs, decorated lunch bags or small plastic bags.

Favors to Buy

There are any number of inexpensive favors that are enjoyed by party-goers and easy on your pocketbook: individually wrapped chocolate mint wafers, instant photos of kids at the party, activity or coloring books, flashlights, and miniature cards, to name a few. For a really great A-to-Z list of ideas, turn the page!

FAVORITE FAVORS FROM A to Z

A—Autograph books, action figure, airplanes *(plastic, balsa wood or paper)*, animal cracker boxes.

B—Bubbles and blowers, bubble bath, baseball cards, batons, barrettes, buttons, bandanas, balloons, banners, bells, bug boxes, bracelets, bike acessories *(reflectors, bells, streamers, license plates, clickety clackety things)*, books *(comic, golden, paperback, coloring, individualized, activity)*, balls *(nerf, super, soccer, rubber, base, foot, whiffle)*.

C—Cars *(mini, plastic)*, checkers set, cookie cutters, crayons, candy, cheer leading pom-poms, chopsticks, compass, costume make-up, crowns, chalk, craft project materials.

D—Dolls, doll clothes, drawing paper, dominos, dice, dimes, dried foods, decals, deck of cards.

E—Earrings *(stick-on, plastic, make-your-own)*, erasers, egg, the plasic kind.

F—Flowers t*(live, silk, plastic)*, frisbees, fruit, frames, flash cards, flags, fans, fishing poles, fortune cookies.

G—Gum *(bubble, sugarless)*, goldfish and bowls, gemstones/minerals/rocks, games, gift certificates *(to fast food restaurants, amusement parks, etc)*.

H—Hairbrush, comb and mirror sets, hair bows, hula hoops, head bands, hats, horns.

I—Ice cream certificates, instant photos.

J—Jacks, jump rope, jewelry, jumbo paper clips, jellybeans and jujubes.

K—Kaleidoscopes, kid-sized kitchen tools, kites, key chains, kazoos.

L—Locks with keys or padlocks *(give combinations to mom also)*, lollipops, light sticks.

M—Magnets, markers, masks, magic tricks, marbles, magnifying glassess, Magic Slates, mugs, mirrors, megaphone, modeling clay.

N—Necklaces, noisemakers, nuts, nickels, note pads.

O—Origami paper.

P—Periscopes, pennants, pom poms, pet rocks, punch balls, pin wheels, pencils, pencil grips, pens, paper dolls, potted plants, puzzles, purses, playing cards, paints and brushes, pennies, pony tail holders, post cards.

Q—Quarters, Quartz and other rocks.

R—Ruler, rings, ribbons, records, rockets.

S—Seeds, stationery, shoe strings, straws *(fancy, twisted, striped, bendable)*, stickers, stars, scissors, stencils, sun glasses, sweat bands, sport sox, sand bucket and shovels.

T—Toothbrushes, trucks, tops, tapes, telescopes.

U—Umbrellas *(paper)*.

V—Visors, vegtables, African violets, videos *(inexpensive cartoon or duplicate of party video)*

W—Whistles, wands, water toys.

X—E-X-plorer equipment, e-X-ercise accessories *(sweatbands, leg warmers)*.

Y—Yo-yos.

Z—Zoo full of animals *(plastic, stuffed, wind up, inflatable, crackers)*

from Peggy Middendorf, Laurenceville, GA

• Fill party bags with small wrapped candies, a box of animal crackers, individually wrapped chocolate mint wafers, pieces or packs of sugarless gum (for older children).

• Save shopping time and, perhaps, money by buying items in sets such as 4-or 6-pack sets of modeling clay, small toys, metal or plastic cars, or other little items and dividing them among the separate favor bags.

• Buy (or make) modeling clay and place in individual plastic bags. Tie several bags together with yarn. The children can play with the clay at the party or take it home. Attach a cookie cutter for even more fun.

Party Supplies by Mail

These companies sell a wide variety of decorations or party favors by mail order. Call for their free catalogs.

U.S. Toy
1227 E 119th Street
Grandview, MO 64030
1-800-255-6124

Dover Publications
31 East 11th Street
Mineola, NY 11501
(516) 294-7000
Activity Books Catalog

M & N International, Inc.
13680 West Laurel Drive
Lake Forest, IL 60045
(847) 680-4700
Ask for Party Catalog

Oriental Trading Co.
P.O. Box 3407
Omaha, NE 68103
1-800-228-0475 or
1-800-228-2269

Favors You Can Create

• Make your own sticker books by stapling several sheets of waxed paper together and putting one sticker on each page. The stickers can be reused and moved from page to page.

• Personalize wide barrettes with tiny self-stick letters, or decorate them with small stickers.

• Decorate borders of inexpensive picture frames with stickers, or personalize frames with permanent markers. Insert instant photos taken at the party into frames as favors to take home.

• Roll up several pages from a "just-add-water-and-paint" coloring book, tie with a ribbon, and attach a paintbrush.

• Weave ribbon through plastic grocery strawberry baskets to hold favors. Add a handle made of pipe cleaners. These pretty baskets can also serve as table decorations.

One of the most popular favors we ever gave out was a live goldfish. We included a small bowl with gravel, food, etc. We got the idea from our party theme, which was fishing.
Leslie Melamed, Deephaven, MN

Distributing Favors

• Distribute the party or loot bags at the very end of the party, just as each guest is going out the door. Make sure the bags are clearly marked with the children's names.

• Wrap identical favors and put them in a large bag or box and use the "grab bag" method as the guests depart.

• Fasten an instant photo you've taken of each child to each favor bag, and let the kids identify their own bags that way.

• Place an open decorated box on the table as a centerpiece. Put a favor for each child in the box, with a streamer tied to the favor and leading to each child's place at the table. Let the children pull their streamer with its attached favor as they sit down.

Prizes: Yes or No?

If your birthday child is a toddler, you won't need prizes—the children are too young for real games and usually aren't able to handle the idea of someone else carrying off the treasure. Even for preschoolers prizes may cause problems. At least avoid prizes for 2nd and 3rd place winners. Children over 7 love games and will probably be disappointed if there are no prizes for winners. If you do give prizes, try to make sure that everyone gets one.

• Consider non-material prizes for young children, such as being first in the next game, sitting next to the birthday child at the table or during the present-opening ceremony, or receiving a round of applause from the group. Try setting up teams and keeping track of the points earned so the entire team can be rewarded when the game ends.

• Use your imagination to award prizes to non-winners: the best laugh, the hardest tries, the best sport, the greenest shirt, the first to touch his nose, etc.. Anything to win a prize!

• Provide a grab bag of inexpensive prizes for things like "just because everyone played the games so well!".

• Self-stick badges and/or colored ribbons make flashy prizes for winners. You can buy them in any office supply store.

What Games and Activities Can I Plan?

Unless you work with preschoolers on a regular basis, what will be newest for you is organizing and entertaining small children en masse. It's not tricky or hard, but it does take preplanning. Children left to their own devices usually don't come up with constructive fun activities—at least not ones whose creativity you'll appreciate.

Your game plan needs to be written out, as well as thought out, in advance (see *Your Activity Planner*, page 85). It is important for you to tailor party activities to your child's level of development. When in doubt about the appropriateness of an activity, you have your own test market—try it out on your child! Do your testing well in advance of the party. Above all, remember that young children like familiar games and activities. Too much creativity on your part could actually be a drawback.

*PICK GAMES YOUR CHILD LIKES AND IS GOOD AT.
NOTHING IS HARDER ON A CHILD THAN HAVING
TO PLAY SOMETHING AT ONE'S OWN PARTY THAT
HE OR SHE CAN'T DO WELL OR DO AT ALL!*

Which to Choose, What to Do?

Let your child have some say in this but be ready to offer choices or make suggestions instead of leaving the question open-ended.

Some games take too long to play, others don't take long enough. If you're dealing with toddlers, forget the games and read aloud to them, have a sing-along, or just let them play. At 3, children are ready for more activity, but you should include many of the easier games you'd use for a 2-year-old. 4-year-olds are open to a wider variety of activities.

• Play games that involve all the children and de-emphasize competition and prizes. Children can't handle defeat until they're about 7 years old (if ever!).

• Avoid elimination games. Otherwise, as children are eliminated you'll have to find something else to amuse them. The same goes for games that involve only one child at a time (like Pin the Tail on the Donkey, for example). When a child's turn is over, he or she often loses interest. You may want to set up a second activity to take place alongside the first game.

• Remember that races stimulate aggressiveness, and it may be hard to calm the children down afterward. However, if you have lots of running space or are outdoors, races can be great for burning off energy. Relay races can encourage positive team spirit and camaraderie.

• Don't get involved in messy activities with more than a couple of children unless you're outdoors where finger painting or sandbox play can be fun for all involved.

• Remember that most inside games can also be played outdoors but that the reverse isn't always true. If you plan too many outdoors-only activities, think about what happens to your party if it turns out to be a rainy day!

• Don't worry too much about games being too simple for older children. Most kids like to "go back" to familiar games and may be able to help teach younger children how to play.

Be Prepared!

- Fill a box or basket with everything you'll need for each game or activity, and stack the boxes right in the game area.

- Keep an index card with all games (and rules) written down in the order in which they are to be played.

- Consider wearing a whistle around your neck as a way of getting the attention of even the overly-excited kids.

- Plan activities that are both simpler and more difficult than you think the kids can handle. That way you'll be prepared if you've misjudged the children's abilities or moods.

- Check with your library for books of suitable games, or talk with your child's nursery school teacher or a daycare worker for other favorite games the children all know how to play.

You might want to modify games to be appropriate to the season or to complement your theme. Consider games which feature clowns, hero figures, witches, reindeer, or bunnies, whatever seems right.

One fun activity that also serves as a party remembrance is to tape-record interviews with the children. They delight in hearing themselves on tape. Avoid visible microphones, if possible, as they might be "eaten" or fought over. Questions to use for interviews can include, *"Why do we celebrate birthdays?, How old are you?, Describe what you look like."* If your own child is overwhelmed by the day's events and prefers to tape his or her interview after the guests are gone, go with that.

*JUST AS THE BIRTHDAY CHILD IS ENTITLED TO THE
FIRST PIECE OF CAKE, HE OR SHE SHOULD
BE THE FIRST TO BE "IT" IN A GAME.*

Minimize Stress for the Sake of Success

• The order in which you do things is important. You should alternate active activities with reasonably quiet ones to avoid either chaos or boredom.

• If you have ten or more guests, divide them into two groups for games. Let your helper play with one group while you help the others. Children aren't good at waiting and watching. This tactic will also prevent unoccupied children from wandering.

• Plan more games than you think you'll need in case some of them turn out to be too hard or don't appeal to the children. You may also be surprised at the speed with which some games can be played. One professional party planner suggests planning at least twice as many games as you expect to have time for.

• Don't feel that you have to play all the games that you planned. If a game seems unpopular, go on to the next one. Take your cues from the kids. If they are having fun with something, let them continue: if they're bored, move on.

Don't force an unwilling child to play a game. The younger the guests, the more likely it is that some will not want to play every game. Have an alternative available, such as coloring or putting a puzzle together.

Suggested activities and games are grouped as follows:
- Arts and Crafts Activities
- Food-Related Activities
- Musical Games and Finger Plays
- Active Games *(Competitive; Noncompetitive)*
- Quiet(er) Games *(Competitive; Noncompetitive)*
- Storytelling

YOUR ACTIVITY PLANNER

Craft Activities: *Time Estimate:*

_____   _____
_____   _____
_____   _____
_____

Craft Materials on Hand: *Need to Buy:*

_____   _____
_____   _____
_____   _____
_____   _____
_____

Games & Entertainment: *Time Estimate:*

_____   _____
_____   _____
_____   _____
_____   _____
_____   _____
_____

Other Activities   *Time Estimate:*

_____   _____
_____   _____
_____   _____

 Arrival Activity: Party-Ending Activity:

_____   _____

Other possible items needed:
   records/tapes   record/tape player
   toys   books
   songbooks   games

Arts and Crafts Activities

Crafts allow equal participation by all, without competition, and children are always proud to have something to "show-and-tell" about themselves, especially when the party is given for another.

Arranging a craft project for the children to do as an arrival activity instead of leaving them to initiate unorganized play can get your party off to a good start.

The craft activities listed here are appropriate for children 2 and over; they can be modified for different ages. Pick what fits your interests, your party theme, or your child's preferences.

T-Shirt Fun

Buy the most inexpensive plain white T-shirts you can find and let the children decorate them with crayons or permanent markers. Crayons usually need to be heat-set, so send home directions with the shirt. If the kids are old enough and you have adequate help for supervision, give them iron-on patches for fancier shirts. Or let them make hand-print shirts by first pressing their palms in fabric paint and then pressing their palms on the T-shirt. Letter their names on their shirts with a marker.

Hand-Decorated Handkerchiefs

Give each child a plain white, inexpensive handkerchief. Have a large assortment of crayons on hand, and let the children decorate the handkerchiefs by pressing the crayons hard to get the wax into the cloth. To fix the colors, place each finished handkerchief between two damp cloths and press with a warm iron.

No-Mess Finger Painting

For each child, put ¼ cup of liquid laundry starch and 3 table-spoons of powdered tempera paint into a large re-sealable plastic bag. Squeeze out the air before locking the bag and seal it tightly with a piece of masking tape. Squeeze the bag gently to blend the paint and starch. The kids put the bags flat on a table and use fingers or hands to create pictures, "erasing" by smoothing out the bags. Try having them do it to music.

Rock Painting

Let each child make a paperweight to take home, using small, smooth rocks and tempera paint. Mix some liquid starch with the paint to give it a consistency that adheres to the rocks. Be ready to help with suggestions—faces, flowers, animals—and encourage the kids to paint the backs as well as the fronts of their creations.

Macaroni Necklace by Pattern

In a bowl, mix 2 or more kinds of noodles that can be strung. On cards, draw patterns of different arrangements of the noodles. Give each child a shoelace with a knot at one end and have him or her string the noodles following the pattern on the card. Younger children can work "free style." When the shoestrings are filled, tie the ends together to form necklaces. Another variation for a stringing assortment is to use 1-inch to 2-inch pieces cut from drinking straws in combination with large beads.

Tin Can Planters

Collect an assortment of clean small cans (tuna fish, etc.). Put a layer of pebbles in the bottom of each for drainage, then fill almost full of potting soil. Let the children plant small seedlings such as pansies or marigolds in the cans and pat down soil around them. Another variation of this idea is simply to let the children plant seeds that will sprout after they are home a few days. Marigold and bean seeds are two good choices.

Fancy Planters

Supply fine gravel or very small pebbles (or small seeds or yarn), white glue, and a small clay flowerpot for each child. Coat the outside of pots and one side of each pebble with glue, and when it's tacky, press the pebbles onto the pot in patterns or designs. (Cotton balls dipped in nail polish remover will help take glue off the children's fingers.) Let the pots dry thoroughly before filling or planting. A plastic margarine tubs or the bottom half of a milk carton works equally well as a pot.

Vegetable Bin Folks

Put out an assortment of round and oval root vegetables, such as potatoes and rutabagas, and a quantity of buttons, fabric scraps, yarn, lace, sequins, cotton balls, and such. Let the children create bodies by stacking smaller vegetables on larger ones and connecting them with toothpicks. Dress the creatures by gluing on the scraps, trimming the clothes with the small items. Buttons are good for eyes, yarn for hair, cotton for beards.

Bean Bags

Give each guest an old sock, a handful of dried beans or corn, and a sewing needle with a large eye, threaded with yarn knotted at one end. Set up a community workspace with scissors, glue, a stapler, felt-tip markers, and assorted scraps of fabric, felt, ribbon, and such. Show the kids how to cut off the toe end of the sock, fill it with the beans or corn and staple or sew it up tightly. They can decorate their bean bags with the materials as they wish, then play a game of bean bag toss.

Decorating Balloons

Supply plenty of blown-up balloons, tempera paints, brushes, glue, and as varied an assortment of fabric scraps, bits of colored or gift wrap paper, feathers, glitter, ribbon, and the like as you can put together. The kids will do the rest.

A Doll Like Me!

Cut child-sized lengths of paper from a big roll of wrapping paper or newsprint (your local newspaper or paper goods store may be able to supply this). Have each child lie down on the paper and trace around the outside of the child's body with a marker or soft lead pencil. (Children over 5 can outline each other.) Give the children markers or crayons so they can draw in facial features and clothing. Supply fabric scraps, buttons, etc., for decoration.

Easy Puppets

Cut the fingers off old gloves and let the children decorate them, using marking pens, yarn, and scraps to make finger puppets. Follow the same idea with old socks to make hand puppets.

Puppet-in-a-Cup

Give each child a cup cut from an egg carton, a regular paper cup, and a wooden popsicle stick. Let the kids use crayons to draw faces on the egg carton cups and give them scraps of yarn and cotton balls to glue on for hair. Poke holes in the tops of the heads and push the popsicle sticks through, taping the sticks securely on the insides. Poke holes in the bottoms of the paper cups and put the other ends of the sticks through them. When the kids push the sticks up and down, the puppets will pop up from the cups and then retreat back down into them.

Play Dough

A batch of homemade play dough made up in advance can entertain guests at the beginning, middle, or end of the party. Supply re-sealable plastic bags so the children can take their creations home. Or give them a ball of dough to take home to play with. These recipes will make enough for 3 to 4 children.

No-Cook Play Dough

1¹/₂ cup white flour
¹/₂ cup salt
2 tablespoons oil

Mix ingredients and add colored water, a little at a time, until the mixture is the consistency of bread dough.

Stove-Top Play Dough

2 cups (1 lb box) baking soda
1 cup corn starch
1 ¹/₄ cups cold water—
with food coloring added

Cook and stir over a medium heat until thickened. After 10-15 minutes when it feels like moist mashed potatoes, spread on a plate or piece of foil until it's cool enough to handle. Store up to 1 week in an airtight container in the refrigerator.

Sewing Cards

Use plastic lids from cans. Make holes ahead of time with a hole puncher, either around the edge of the lid or to form a design. Provide needles and yarn or shoelaces for decorating the lids.

Light Switch Art

Buy plastic light switch plates at the hardware store and let the children decorate them with stickers or markers. Each child can design one to take home for his or her own bedroom.

Food-Related Activities

Food crafts are fun to make and fun for the children to "show-and-tell"; in addition, they can be good to eat...in spite of all the handling. Use your imagination as you come up with ideas for ways to use food as a craft material!

Food Sculpture

To create a piece of sculpture from different foods, the following foods are suitable as "handles": pretzel sticks, tooth picks, popsicle sticks, wooden or plastic ice cream spoons, straws, or pipe cleaners. To stick on the handles in any desired arrangement: pineapple chunks, sliced apples, pears, or any other fruit; berries, grapes; mini-marshmallows, gumdrops; raisins or other dried fruits; pitted or stuffed olives; cherry tomatoes or chunks of other vegetables; cheese cubes or chunks of lunch meat. The kids will design the "art" for themselves!

Edible Play Dough

You can make a batch of dough (with or without your child's help) before the party and have it ready for the guests to play with and then eat during the party.

Make-and-Eat Play Dough

2 cups flour
4 cups oatmeal
1 cup water
1 cup white corn syrup
1 cup peanut butter
1 ¼ cups nonfat
  powdered milk
1 ¼ cups sifted
  confectioners' sugar

Combine flour and oatmeal in a blender and "grind" together for 30 seconds. Add 1 cup water and knead. Add corn syrup, peanut butter, nonfat powdered milk, and confectioners' sugar. Combine and knead well. Add more flour and/or powdered milk if the dough is too sticky to knead. Put out bowls of chocolate, butterscotch, or carob chips, sunflower seeds, and   s h e l l e d peanuts for the kids to decorate their creations and to make them tastier.

Variation: Mix 1 16-oz jar peanut butter with 6 tablespoons honey. Add nonfat dry milk and/or flour until the peanut butter loses its stickiness. Carob or chocolate powder can be added.

Edible Jewelry

Give the children blunt needles threaded with string and provide bowls of anything stringable: mini-marshmallows, Cheerios®, licorice, raisins, olives, dried fruits, popcorn. Or use a piece of twine or a string of licorice for threading Cheerios®, Fruit Loops, or Lifesavers®. If nutrition is a concern, you can steam various vegetables until just softened enough so the needles can pierce through them to make a veggie necklace or bracelet.

Bobbing for Doughnuts

Hang doughnuts by string from the ceiling or a clothesline and let the kids "bob" for them using their mouths but not their hands (better be prepared for some cheating!).

Bread Dough Pretzels

Divide a loaf of thawed, kneaded frozen bread dough among six or eight children. Let them roll the pieces with their hands into long, narrow ropes and twist or braid or fashion them into pretzel shapes or any other shape. Brush with beaten egg (optional). Bake at 325 degrees for 15 minutes. Creations can be eaten while fresh and warm just out of the oven or taken home for later.

Peanut People

Supply a big bag of peanuts in the shell and a couple of packages of pipe cleaners. The children can create whole families of peanut people or a zoo of peanut animals by twisting the pipe cleaners around the peanuts for arms, legs, or hats. The kids can then paint on faces with paint or markers.

Food-Filler Spree

Fill a large container with trail mix, a cereal treat, or some other edible bits. Let the kids use spoons to fill their loot bags with as much as they can within a certain count (like 15 seconds, or to the count of 10). Or allow a specific number of handful grabs from the treat sack. (See Chapter 5 for suggestions about decorating cakes, cupcakes, or cookies as a Food-Related Activity.)

Musical Games and Finger Plays

We all remember childhood songs a little differently, just as we all learned slightly different versions of familiar childhood games. Each song listed is one of the accepted versions, but feel free to use the words you grew up singing. The kids certainly won't know or care—in fact, if you listen closely, you may hear them singing a garbled version of their own, anyway!

• Teach little children songs by seating them on the floor in a semicircle and sitting in front of them on a low chair or stool. Keep a copy of the song (or songbook) beside you, in case you forget the words. Don't worry about your lack of singing talent; they're not critical listeners.

• Look for musical movement and games records or tapes like the *Wee Sing* series by Pam Beal and Susan Nipp (published by Price, Stern, Sloan) in mail order catalogs (see page 100).

• Remember when demonstrating finger plays that the children will mirror your actions and use their right hands as you use your left hand, and vice versa.

• Ask the children if they know any songs or finger plays, and let them teach you.

• Be sure that at least some of your songs include action as well as singing, involving the restless children who can't sit still for any length of time.

• Try having a parade with children's musical toys. Or a game of *Follow the Leader*, with the birthday child as the first leader. (Be ready to step in as leader yourself if things get out of hand).

Active Songs

The Mulberry Bush

(Children hold hands and skip around in a circle during the chorus, stopping to act out the words of the song.)

> *Here we go 'round the mulberry bush*
> *the mulberry bush, the mulberry bush.*
> *Here we go 'round the mulberry bush*
> *so early in the morning.*
>
> *This is the way we wash our clothes,*
> *wash our clothes, wash our clothes.*
> *This is the way we wash our clothes*
> *so early Monday morning.*

(*Iron our clothes* for Tuesday, *scrub our floor* for Wednesday, *mend our clothes* for Thursday, *sweep our house* for Friday, *bake our bread* for Saturday, and *sleep in bed* for Sunday)

If You're Happy

If you're happy and you know it,
clap your hands. (Clap, clap!)
If you're happy and you know it,
clap your hands. (Clap, clap!)
If you're happy and you know it
then your face will surely show it.
If you're happy and you know it,
clap your hands. (Clap, clap!)

(Subsequent verses can substitute for *clap your hands*: *stamp your feet, turn around, swing your arms, hug yourself*, and *nod your head*—or whatever you invent!)

Head, Shoulders, Knees, and Toes

(Sung to the tune of *There Is a Tavern in the Town* while the children put their hands on each part of the body as it is mentioned.)

Head, shoulders, knees, and toes,
Knees and toes;
Head, shoulders, knees, and toes,
Knees and toes and
Eyes and ears and mouth and nose,
Head, shoulders, knees, and toes, knees and toes.

I'm a Little Teapot

I'm a little teapot, short and stout.
This is my handle, (put hand on hip)
This is my spout. (bend other arm up)
When I get all steamed up, then I shout,
Tip me over (bend to the side)
and pour me out !"

The Farmer in the Dell

The farmer in the dell,　　*The farmer takes a wife,*
The farmer in the dell,　　　*The farmer takes a wife,*
Heigh ho the derry-o,　　　*Heigh ho the derry-o,*
The farmer in the dell.　　　*The farmer takes a wife.*

The wife takes a child . . .
The child takes a nurse . . .
The nurse takes a dog . . .
The dog takes a cat . . .
The cat takes a mouse . . .
The mouse takes the cheese . . .
The farmer leaves the dell . . .
The cheese stands alone . . .

(Play with a minimum of ten children standing in a circle around the "Farmer." Children are pulled into the center of the circle one by one and then go back to their places one by one, leaving the "Cheese" all alone in the center. The children clap along to the last verse, which ends the game.)

Ring Around the Rosie

(Children join hands and skip around in a circle, falling down at the end of the song—best for very young children.)

> *Ring around the rosie,*
> *A pocket full of posies,*
> *Ashes, ashes,*
> *We all fall down!*

Drop the Hanky

(Have the children form a large circle facing inward. The child who is "it" holds a handkerchief and walks slowly around the outside of the circle while the children sing:)

> *A tisket, a tasket, a green and yellow basket,*
> *I wrote a letter to my love, and on the way I dropped it.*
> *I dropped it, I dropped it, the green and yellow basket,*
> *A little child picked it up and put it in his pocket.*

(The child who is "it" may drop the hanky behind any child in the circle, then takes off running around the circle to sit in the vacated spot before being tagged. If the first child is tagged, he or she becomes "it" for the next round.)

Quiet(er) Songs

Inky Dinky Spider

Inky Dinky Spider
Went up the water spout.
   (wiggle fingers to look like a spider)
Down came the rain
And washed the spider out.
   (hold hands high and bring down like falling rain)
Out came the sun
And dried up all the rain
   (extend hands over head in a circle)
and Inky Dinky Spider
Crawled up the spout again.
   (wiggle fingers to look like a spider)

I Have Two...

(Children point to each part of the body as it's named.)

> *I have two little eyes*
> *That open and close.*
> *I have two little ears*
> *And one little nose.*
> *I have two soft cheeks,*
> *And one little chin.*
> *I have two lips that*
> *close my teeth in.*

Hickory Dickory Dock

(Children use hands to act out mouse up, mouse down, and a single finger to indicate the clock striking.)

> *Hickory dickory dock*
> *The mouse ran up the clock*
> *The clock struck one*
> *The mouse ran down*
> *Hickory dickory dock*

Active Games (*Competitive*)

When you're planning birthday party games, remember that kids love tradition. You may think, "But they play that game at *every* party!" Your child will want it anyway because he or she knows the rules and likes the game. If it really is a game that's played at every birthday party, then the party won't be complete without it. It's a good idea to avoid team games or scavenger hunts until the children are at least seven or eight.

Pin the (_____) on the (_____)

There's always *The Tail on the Donkey*, but you could vary it with *Backpack on the Hiker*, or *Balloon on the Clown's Nose*. Your imagination and your willingness to find or draw a large picture are your only limitations. (Yes, you can buy a commercial *Pin the Tail on the Donkey* game.) Have more than one blindfold handy and at least one more adult to help. The blindfold should not be so tight that the child can't see his or her feet. Don't turn a child around more than twice; the blindfold will be disorienting enough.

Although small children (under age 3) may be frightened of the blindfold), this game is an old favorite and most kids love it. To be on the safe side, use small pieces of masking tape instead of thumbtacks or straight pins to attach the objects to the picture. Don't forget to put the child's name on his or her "tail."

Duck, Duck, Goose (a.k.a. *Grey Duck* or *Drop the Handkerchief*)

"It" walks around the outside of a circle of seated children, tapping each on the head and saying "duck" to all but one, who's "goose." "Goose" gets up and chases "It." When "It" is caught, he or she sits down and "goose" becomes "It." As a variation "It" drops a handkerchief or other small item behind the back of one child (see page 98)—a bit more difficult to play because the children have to look behind them as "It" passes to see the dropped item.

Drop the Clothespin

Give each child three or four clothespins or other small items (tiny plastic toys, peanuts, pennies, wrapped candies). The children take turns kneeling on a chair to drop the items over the chair back into a hat or basket (not always so easy.) The children could keep the items that go into the basket or you could give a prize to the winner, the child who gets the most objects into the basket.

Bean Bag Tosses

A target for the bean bag toss can be as easy as a basket or hat or as challenging as the open mouth of a clown you've drawn and cut out from the side of a cardboard box. You could also hang a big bell from a tree branch and have the kids try to ring it by hitting it with a toss of the beanbag.

Balloon Races

Have the kids hop to the finish line with balloons between their knees. Or let them try to keep balloons in the air by swatting at them with their hands as they walk across a room. Or give each child a different color balloon and have them walk to the finish line while kicking their balloons ahead of them; or crawl on their hands and knees, pushing the balloons ahead with their noses. You should have plenty of replacement balloons on hand!

Balloon Break

Tie blown-up balloons to each child's ankles. The object is to break each other's balloons and protect their own from being broken. The last to have an unbroken balloon is the winner. (Best to play this one without shoes!)

Mother, May I ?

The children line up, facing "Mother," who stands 10 or 15 feet away. "Mother" calls each child in turn by name and says, "You may take one giant step" (or 2 baby steps, or 3 hops, or anything "Mother" wishes). The child must answer, "Mother, may I?" and receive permission ("Yes, you may") before proceeding. Anyone who fails to ask goes back to the starting line. The child who reaches "Mother" first is the next "Mother". In another version of the game, the children can try to sneak steps while "Mother" isn't looking, but if caught, they must return to the starting line.

Velcro Toss

A target toss game using Velcro® balls is a good game for children of all ages. Young children can count how many balls hit and stick to the board; older children can keep track of their score.

Wheelbarrow Race

Separate the children into pairs. One child holds the legs of the other, who walks on his or her hands. When the pair reaches the goal line, they switch positions and go back to the starting line. The pair that returns to the starting line first wins.

Simon Says

Have "Simon" face a line of standing children and give a command: "Simon says touch your toes." The whole group follows the instruction unless the phrase "Simon says" is left out, in which case they should not move. Anyone who does move is "out" and the game continues, with varying commands being given until only one child is left. Avoid the problem of what to do with those who are "out" by having anyone who makes an error go to one side or to the other end of the line and continue to play until one child reaches the head of the line. You might want to substitute the birthday child's name for "Simon."

Spud

This game is played with a large group and a ball soft enough to throw at other players. The players stand in a close group while one player throws the ball straight up in the air and calls out the name of one of the players. That player then catches the ball and yells "Freeze" and all the other players must stop right where they are. The player with the ball then throws the ball at another player. If hit, that player is assigned the letter "S". When a player has picked up all four letters "S-P-U-D," he or she is out of the game. If the thrower doesn't hit anyone, that person picks up a letter. If a player is hit, he or she gets the ball and the turn to throw it at another player. If a player is thrown at and missed, he or she picks up the ball, throws it in the air, and calls out a new name. Play the game until the first player is out with "S-P-U-D", or until all are out but one.

Relay Races

Competitive and active, yet tempered by teamwork, relay races are for children over age 4 and if there are at least six or more children at the party. Teams can race with an egg on a spoon, or hopping on one foot or walking backward. A favorite race is the clothes bag relay: have two bags of similar clothes (a hat, a big shirt, old shoes, mittens, etc.). A child on each team runs to a bag, puts on all the clothes—no need to tie or button! Then the child takes off all the clothes, puts them back in the bag, runs back to the team, and the next team member takes off to repeat the process. First team to finish wins.

The Obstacle Course

For 5 or 6-year-olds, create an obstacle course that each child must complete while being timed. Set up safe barriers where the children can run, jump, crawl or walk a narrow beam in about a minute or two. Keep the time short so those not participating don't get bored while waiting for their turn.

Shoe Mix-Up

Tell the children to remove their shoes and place them in a pile, then mix the shoes up. At a signal the children race for their shoes and put them on as fast as they can. This race is best for 4-year-olds and up, especially if tying shoelaces is a requirement.

Active Games *(Noncompetitive)*

London Bridge Is Falling Down

Have the children stand in a circle, with two of them making an arch by facing each other with upraised arms. As music plays, the children walk through the arch. When the music stops, the two forming the arch drop their arms and try to "capture" the child going through. When two have been caught, they form another arch for the players to go through. When two more are caught, they form a third arch, and so on until only one player is left.

Musical Chairs

There is a noncompetitive version of the familiar game in which the player who can't find a vacant chair when the music stops is out. (With the old version you end up with a lot of kids who have nothing to do while the game goes on.) Instead, play the music, take a chair away when it stops, but have the child who doesn't have a chair sit on the lap of one who does. Continue until all the children are on one chair, or on each other. (This can get to be rowdy but lots of fun!)

Tag Games

Assign one "safety" position, such as squatting or holding the hands above the head, in which a player cannot be caught. If the game moves too slowly, limit the "safe" position to 5 seconds. Or have any person caught join hands with "It" and help catch the others until all are joined. Or play "Everybody's It," where everyone runs around tagging each other. Anyone tagged must stand still, with hands on head, until everyone has been tagged.

Musical Laps

Have the children stand in a circle, each with their hands on the hips of the child ahead. While music plays, the children walk around the circle; when the music stops, each sits back in the lap of the one behind, while continuing to hold the hips of the one ahead. The game usually ends in giggles and everybody wins! (This game might be best played without shoes.)

Popping for Prizes

Slip small papers with numbers on them—one for each child at the party—into balloons, then blow up the balloons. Have the kids sit on the balloons to break them and get the papers out. The numbers determine their prizes. (You may want to keep a pin on hand to pop the balloon of any child who doesn't want to sit on it.) To carry the game a step further: have one child leave the room and let the others hide his or her prize. When the child returns, the kids can give clues by saying, "You're warm, You're cold, You're hot," or by humming loudly for "hot" and softly for "cold."

Body Parts

Have the children form a circle around you. (You can give each one a carpet square to stand on, and send it home as a favor.) When you touch a part of your body without speaking aloud the children do the same. Or you can call out the name of a part of your body as you touch it, and the children do the same. Or you can touch one part of your body with another (toe to toe, arm to leg, ear to shoulder, toe to nose, wrist to lips, hand to eye, etc.). *Variation*: Give each child a balloon to touch the body parts and to move under, over, between legs, in front, behind, etc.

Spin the Bottle

Have the children sit in a circle. Place a rolled-up message (words or pictures) in a bottle, spin the bottle, and when it stops the person it points to takes out the message and does what it says. Message ideas: hug someone, rub your tummy, hop on one foot, shake hands with everyone, make the sound of the animal pictured, etc.

"Do as I Do" Dance

With brisk music playing and the children standing in a circle, the first child starts the dance with a single gesture such as raising one arm. The other children follow suit. The next child repeats the motion and adds another, like stamping a foot. Everyone repeats both gestures; the dance continues with each child in turn adding a new motion and everyone repeating all of the gestures.

African Safari

Build a maze or obstacle course for "animals" to traverse. Each child chooses to be a favorite animal. Use large open boxes to create tunnels; a board can become a precarious bridge over a river; stuffed animals can become dangerous jungle animals to avoid or jump over. Once successfully through the maze, the children could be rewarded with animal crackers.

Quiet(er) Games *(Competitive)*

Memory

Place an assortment of small household items on a tray, a few items for young children, more for older ones. Let the children study the tray for a few minutes, then cover it. Older children then write down the names of all the items they can remember. For younger children, keep several items in a bag, alternating items on the tray for the children to guess. The one who remembers the most items wins. *Memory* can also be played as a team game.

Variation: Put the items in a bag and have the kids feel them before trying to remember what they felt.

Guess What I Am

Fill a basket or bowl with pictures of different animals. The child who is *"it"* picks a picture out of the bowl or basket and must then imitate the animal until someone guesses what kind it is. The first child to guess correctly is *"it"* next, and the game can continue until everyone has had a turn.

Guess the Sound

Sometime before the party make a tape of some common sounds. Play the tape at the party and ask the children to guess what sounds they're hearing. Examples are: the car starting, the toilet flushing, a clock ticking, a washing machine running.

Beginner's Bingo

Make up grid cards (like *Tic-Tac-Toe*) from heavy cardboard on which you print numbers from 1 to 6 in random order within the boxes. You will need a die and pennies or buttons for markers. The first player throws the die and counts the dots, then covers that number on the card with a marker. The players take turns throwing the die. The first player to cover a row horizontally, vertically, or diagonally (or the entire card) is the winner.

L'Egg Hunt

Place a basket of empty L'Eggs® pantyhose containers in the center of a circle of children. One container holds a ribbon. Each child chooses an egg from the basket and opens it. The child who gets the egg with the ribbon wins a prize. This can be turned into a noncompetitive game by placing a different colored ribbon in each container. A blue ribbon, for instance, lets a child reach into a blue prize grab bag, a red ribbon, a red prize grab bag, and so on.

Unwrap the Package

Unwrap the Package is a game for older children. Wrap a small favor in several layers of different wrapping paper. The children sit in a circle and pass the package around as music plays. When the music stops, the child holding the package unwraps one layer, the music starts and the package is passed to the next child. The child who removes the last layer of wrapping keeps the favor.

Quiet Games *(Noncompetitive)*

Guess the Leader

The children sit in a circle on the floor, and "It" leaves the room while those in the circle select a leader who starts and changes simple motions (pulling an ear, rubbing an eyebrow, twisting a lock of hair). The others copy the leader, and "It" tries to guess who the leader is. The leader and "It" change places after three guesses. The game continues until everyone has had a turn at being both "It" and the leader.

Tell Me If I'm Wrong

An adult starts the game by selecting a category of things children are familiar with like food, animals, furniture, etc. Speak fairly slowly and call out a number of items, then throw in one that doesn't fit ("banana" in a list of animals, for example). The children shout "No" or raise their hands or shake their heads when a word that doesn't fit is called out. Let the children volunteer to take turns being the caller, but be available to help, if necessary.

Fishing for Favors

Before the party, cut simple fish shapes, about 3" long, from heavy paper and attach a paper clip to each. Write a number on each fish, one for each child who will be at the party. Make fishing poles from sticks and string and attach a magnet to the end of each string. The children "fish" until each one catches a fish. The number of fish caught determines the prize. Everybody wins.

Doggie, Doggie, Where's Your Bone?

One child is "It" and sits in the center of a circle of children. "It" closes his or her eyes, and one child is given the "bone" (any small item will do). All the children sit with their hands held behind their backs, and "It" has three chances to guess who has the bone. If the child who is "It" guesses who has the bone, that child holding the bone then becomes "It."

Cotton Balls

Blindfold one child and give him or her a cup and spoon. Spread newspaper on the floor and put 12 to 15 cotton balls all around. The blindfolded player tries to scoop up the cotton balls with the spoon. It's fun to do and fun to watch!

Musical Magic Sack

A grab bag with small, wrapped favors is passed from child to child in a circle while music (tape, radio, or piano) plays. When the music stops, the child who has the sack reaches inside the bag for a prize. Continue to play until all favors are gone. Or everyone can be a winner if you have the children move out of the circle as they win a prize. You may want to ask them all to wait until the game ends before they open the prizes.

Storytelling

Whether you can tell creative stories on your own or you are more comfortable sharing the written word, children delight in sitting around and listening to a story. This works well at any age. But it will not occupy a group as long as it does a single child (there will be too many distractions), so don't plan on more than five to ten minutes for this activity.

- Read favorite stories, especially ones with action.
- Read storybooks with big pictures to show.
- Read with expression and drama. You may even want to have some props to accompany your tale.

Winding Down the Party

Pandora's Box: Opening the Gifts

Selecting the best time to open the presents can be tricky. The children, of course, will want to do this first, but most parents wait until towards the end of the party for various reasons.

Some parents give their own gift to their child before or after the party. Others present it, along with the other gifts, at the party. For what it is worth, do remember that little kids are often more impressed by the size and number of gifts than by their value. To a small child, really good things *don't* come in small packages.

Pretty Packages

The Current Catalog offers many lovely wrapping papers, cards, party bags, stickers, and attractive gift items. For a free copy, write to:

Current Catalog
The Current Building
Colorado Springs, CO 80941
or call 1-800-525-7170

When To Open Gifts

• As each child arrives, show the gift to those who are present and keep things very low-key, downplay the gift-giving and stress friendship and fun. This may be a good practice for toddlers, who are often jealous and want to keep the gifts they bring. Show the gift to those present, then put it away.

• At the beginning of the party, after all the guests have arrived. It's wise to put the gifts away immediately so they won't get broken or have pieces lost before the party's over.

• At the end of the party, just before the guests go home. The advantage to this timing is that the gifts will be intact when the guests leave and letdown may be eliminated. It also lends a bit of mystery and suspense to the day's events.

• After the party, for kids 4 and under. Some feel it's too hard for young party guests not getting presents to watch this.

Gift Opening as an Activity

• Have the guests sit in a semicircle around the birthday child, as nearly equidistant from him or her as possible. (You will probably need a parent helper.)

• Consider having the first present opened be a large plastic garbage bag filled with blown-up balloons. It will be a festive start to the activity and gives the birthday guests something to play with while the gifts are being opened.

• Furnish a receptacle (wastebasket or container) for gift wrappings and ribbons; see to it yourself that these articles—and only these—are discarded right away.

• Stack the gifts by the birthday child and encourage him or her to open them in order instead of rummaging through them for the largest, the brightest, or the best friend's gift. (Good luck!)

• Let each guest hold one present and spin a bottle to select the order in which presents will be opened.

• Read aloud the card and the name of the gift-giver and say something nice about the gift. Hold it up so everyone can see it (for the under-6 set, passing the gift around is unwise—the guests will be tempted to play with it.)

• Let each child hold the present he or she brought and give it to the birthday child in some order.

• The box-within-the-box-within-the box-routine (many boxes have to be opened before reaching the present) is fun for slightly older children of age 6 and up.

• Make a note of the gift and the gift-giver on each card to save for thank-you's later. Or keep a list (or have a helper keep one) as the presents are opened.

• Open only the gifts from the party guests, not those from the family or others who are not present at the party.

The Joy of Receiving

My three-year-old's best gift was lunch bags with her name on them. One of the bags was filled with small sample packages of food, toothpaste, dried fruit, popcorn, etc.

Jeannine Imhoff, Cincinnati, OH

The best and worst gift my three-year-old received was a flashlight. He refused to open any more presents after he opened that one.

Alice Hoffer, McLean, VA

When my son was four, a neighbor gave him a padlock and key for a present. After the party, he said the lock was his favorite gift. He never locked anything up with it; maybe it was enough to know that he could if he wanted to.

Katie Keefer, Edina, MO

Our son's best gift was a "Balloon-O-Gram", which was a bouquet of balloons delivered to the door. He was thrilled.

Kris Taranec, Lake Havasu, AZ

Piñatas

A traditional piñata is a fancy, highly decorative papier-mâché animal filled with candy and small toys. It is the central theme of children's birthday parties throughout Latin America and has become popular in North America as well.

Traditionally the piñata is hung by a rope or a pulley from a branch or hook above the children's heads. When it is on a pulley, the adult can raise or lower it out of reach of a blindfolded child who swings at it with a stick. Each child is usually given three tries to break the piñata. The advantage of the pulley is that the adult can orchestrate, to some degree, when the piñata is broken so that every child can have a turn "at bat."

Older children are blindfolded, steered in the direction of the piñata, and given three or more tries to break it. For younger children, forget the blindfolds—they'll be afraid of them; just hitting the piñata will be enough of a challenge for them. Be sure the piñata is hung securely—pulley, or not.

This activity needs to be closely supervised as children must be kept out of the way of the stick-wielding child. A potential problem could occur if the piñata is partially broken and the contents are dribbling out. Children will rush in to pick up the candy treats while one child is still swinging away!

I don't like the idea of piggy children groveling on the ground grabbing as much as they can. Several children are always too timid to join the ruckus and feel left out of the booty. I prefer to give a small, plastic bag to each child and tell the children, "one bag per child" to eliminate the aggressive struggle to see who can get the most.
Mary McNamara, Deephaven, MN

Unusual piñatas in varied sizes priced from $3.50 to $45 can be ordered from La Piñata, 2 Patio Market, Albuquerque, NM 87104, (505) 242-2400. Call or write for current price list and photos.

Do-It-Yourself Piñatas

• You can make one as plain or as decorative as you wish. The easiest is simply to put several grocery bags inside one another. Decorate or not, fill with candy and toys, and staple or tie securely at the top. Or use a colorful paper shopping bag.

• To make a traditional piñata, start with a thin paste of flour and water. Cut long strips of newspaper—lots of them. Blow up a large balloon, dip the strips one at a time into the paste, and press them onto the balloon. Overlap the strips, covering the balloon securely several times, leaving one end uncovered. Let it dry for 24 hours or more, then pop the balloon and remove it. Fill the piñata with toys and candy and seal the end with more newspaper strips dipped in the flour paste. Decorate your piñata as you wish, making a clown face, a cat face, a jack-o-lantern, whatever. Use tempera paint and any assortment of scraps of paper or cloth. Tie yarn or string around it.

For my son's third birthday, I bought a piñata from a party shop and filled it with goodies (sugarless gum and healthy snacks). We hung it outside and everyone took turns giving it a whack with a broom handle. The piñata was so hard to break that even I had trouble, but no one seemed to mind. It took up a lot of time, taught everyone how to take turns, and we all had a fun surprise at the end when it was finally broken.

Debbie Parnakian, Huntington Beach, CA

Hunt How-To's

Children really love hunts at parties. Even 2-year-olds can enjoy a very simple hunt. Individually wrapped candy, inexpensive favors, and pennies are good treasures. Just be sure that everyone comes back with something and you'll avoid tears and hurt feelings. Keep a few extra items available in case you have a slow "hunter." With a group of older children you could offer a more sophisticated treasure hunt complete with clues.

• Make your outdoor hunt easy on yourself by hiding peanuts (lots of them!) around the yard, keeping in mind that children's eye level is mighty low. Or hide peanuts or pennies in a large, opened bale of hay, or in a sandbox (if you've warned parents to dress their kids in play clothes). *Caution*: Don't hide peanuts or other food outside the night before the party. Squirrels or other animals might win the hunt before it begins!

• Wrap pennies individually in tin foil which makes them easier to spot and takes longer for the children to unwrap.

• Consider a "picture treasure hunt" for a small party—or divide a larger party into teams of three or four children and have several hunts going on at the same time. Use pictures of familiar household items like a TV, a sofa, a refrigerator, a dining room table. Give each team a picture and hide four or five others. On or under the TV set, for example, they will find a picture of a refrigerator, to which they move for the next clue. When they find the hidden treasure, there should be identical prizes for everyone who took part in the hunt.

• Try a "birthday cake hunt" just before it's time to serve the food. In advance, prepare a large puzzle by drawing a picture of a glorious birthday cake on construction paper (the birthday child might help with this) and cutting the drawing into large, obvious shapes. Hide all the pieces in easy-to-find places, and set the kids to hunt for them. When all the pieces are found, the kids will "make the cake" by putting the puzzle together.

• Put clues, either picture or written, in envelopes labeled with each guest's name. The birthday child finds his or hers first, with verbal clues from you, opens it, and leads the whole group to the next clue. Each child in turn is leader, and when the treasure is found, it's divided among all the guests. Or the cake can be the treasure for a hunt just for the birthday child, with one clue leading to another.

End of Party

Towards the end of a party, many children (including the birthday child) may be overstimulated. It's a good idea to arrange for one or more quiet, "cooling-off" activities to conclude the party as the children are waiting to be picked up. The activity could be something the children can leave or continue easily, such as coloring. Try to keep departures as happy as possible.

Quiet activities to consider:

• A new selection of coloring books and crayons to use, dot-to-dot books and rub-on transfers.

• An open-ended craft activity such as stencil-tracing or using stamp and ink pads or bead-stringing.

• A group sing-along.

• Watching TV, a rented videotape, or previously taped cartoons, *Sesame Street*, or another children's TV show.

• Playing with your child's other toys. (But check with your child first and put away any toys your child would not like others playing with.)

*It's nice to have a balloon or a treat ready
for a sibling who comes along with a parent.*

Party Letdown

• Be aware that while you probably feel relief and perhaps a bit proud that you've pulled it all off without major problems, your child will probably feel let down when the party is over and everyone has gone home.

• Have in mind something for your child to do after the last guest has left. Put on a quiet record or tape and look over the presents together or read a new book. A comfy lap-snuggle is a good wind-down for you both. (Avoid the rush to clean up.)

• Talk about the party. Find out what he or she liked best and least. Make some notes for next year's party; you may think you'll never forget this day, but by next year you will!

• This can be the time to give your child the additional gifts from those not at the party (packages from relatives, etc.).

• Invite one of your child's favorite guests to stay a little longer to play (it's wise not to let the other guests know—just ask the parent to come for him or her a bit later). Or you might invite a favorite guest and his or her parent to stay after the party for an adult visit over coffee with you while the children play.

• Plan another party to relieve the letdown, even if it's only a birthday party the next day for all the teddy bears in the house.

Thank-You's

• Offer simple thank-you's at the door as the guests leave. Try to remember the gift and make a nice comment about it.

• Let you child make thank-you phone calls or sign his or her name (or draw) on thank-you notes that you write.

• Use a photo taken at the party as a thank-you postcard or note.

• Send adults, especially out-of-town relatives, a photo of the birthday child along with a thank-you note for their gift.

• Encourage your child to thank the guests by phone the next day, but don't insist. An articulate three-year-old may enjoy doing this, but some children, even much older, may balk.

• Some parents enjoy writing notes in the voice of their very young child—certainly a nice thought, but only if that is the type of thing you like to do.

Teaching your young children the importance of showing gratitude for birthday gifts by writing thank-you notes is a good start towards teaching them to show gratitude and appreciation for the thoughtfulness of others. Thank-you note writing is a skill that will serve children throughout their lives—unfortunately it is a skill often neglected these days. Use this opportunity to begin teaching this to your child. Sharing thank-you notes you have received can help him or her understand their importance. You might want to give your child some personalized note paper or postcards as special encouragement.

Chapter 9

For Family Only

If you have a family party in addition to the children's party, be sure to schedule it on a different day to save yourself and your child both from nervous exhaustion.

• Kiss your child good night the night before his or her birthday with, "Good night ("3") year old" and greet the birthday child the next morning with a kiss and a, "Good morning ("4") year old!"

• Have the whole family get up early and gather quietly around the sleeping birthday child's bed. Waken him or her by singing "Happy Birthday" and present a small gift to start the day. Maybe make breakfast in bed part of the birthday tradition.

• Decorate the birthday child's bedroom after you're sure he or she is asleep. Use lots of balloons or the number of balloons for the number of years of the birthday. What an exciting way to wake up on a very special day!

• Decorate the birthday child's place at the breakfast table. Use balloons, crepe paper, or a special plate and place mat.

• Make up a poem, song, or skit in honor of the birthday child. Each member of the family could contribute a piece to it and have a part in presenting it.

• Let the birthday child select the party menu. For some families, each child's birthday menu choice is the same year after year, becoming a tradition.

• Use a special birthday tablecloth for each child—perhaps a plain white one—that can be autographed each year.

• Consider saving the special birthday cake for the family party and serve cupcakes at the children's party, especially if the guests are very young.

• Start family birthday traditions very early. Some ideas: plant a tree or shrub in the yard each year; go on a special outing as a family (to the zoo, a park, a movie); or light a large candle, the same one every year, for just the number of minutes corresponding to the child's age.

• Hang a birthday flag/banner outside the front door so the whole neighborhood will know there is a birthday at your house. (Mom and Dad could be included in this tradition, too!)

• Tape-record each family member recalling one or two favorite times spent with the birthday child during the past year, then play the tape at the party and save it as a keepsake.

• Retell the account of your child's birth each birthday.

• Show home movies of family parties from previous years as after-dinner entertainment. Bring out old photos or show home movies or videos of the birthday child to see how much he or she has grown and changed over the years.

We celebrated all four family birthdays at once with a cookout at noon on a blistering *hot* day with 27 guests! Our son was overwhelmed and so was I! Too many gifts went unnoticed and unappreciated.

Jodi Junge, Bryn Athyn, PA

VIP Treatment for the Birthday Child

• Start the anticipation a week prior to the birthday with a daily countdown of, "five more days to your birthday," "four more days to your birthday," and so on.

• Consider taking the morning of the birthday off from work to volunteer as a parent helper at school. Perhaps you could take the whole day as a vacation day from work and spend the day together, letting your child be in charge of the day.

• Pick school-age children up at school lunch time and take them out to eat. Let them choose where (if it fits the schedule).

• Write a birthday message on your child's bathroom mirror with lipstick—it comes off easily with soap and water.

• Make a special birthday badge from ribbons, lace, sparkles, etc. and mark it with a big number showing your child's age.

• Make a birthday cape to help your child feel regal. You can go all-out and make a royal crown and scepter, too! Or make a cape to incorporate a superhero party theme.

• Set the birthday child's place at the lunch or dinner table with a special place mat, dishes, and glassware. You might want to buy a set reserved just for such occasions.

• Set aside the birthday to make annual fingerprint art or a plaque of your child's handprint. Save them and you'll have graphic proof of your child's growth from year to year.

• Start a birthday book of memories and add to it each year as a wonderful keepsake for your child. Or write an annual letter to your child listing events, achievements and milestones that have occurred throughout the year, as well as photos of that year's birthday party. Another future treasured keepsake!

• Take photos of your child's entire birthday activities from morning wake-up to mealtime, play and bedtime. Put them in a small album for him or her to keep.

• Make a certificate congratulating your child for successfully completing another year of life. You can frame and hang it, and replace it the following year with a new one.

• Buy a gift that can be added to each year such as a string of add-a-pearls or a charm bracelet or a collection of some kind. It can start a lovely tradition.

• Gift wrap *everything* feasible for the birthday child—hairbrush, apple, juice cup, hat and mittens, etc.

• Commemorate a birthday by donating $10 to the U.S. Forest Service's Plant-A-Tree Program. For information: write the U.S. Forest Service, P.O. Box 96090, Washington, DC 20090.

• Order a frameable scroll 11" x 14" documenting the historical highlights of the day of your child's birth, includes name and an illustrated border. $11.95 plus $2.95p/h from GREAT DAYS, 4191-12 Carpinteria Ave, Carpinteria, CA 93014, (800) 447-7817.

I take the day off from work so my daughter and I can spend the whole day together. First we go to the doctor for her annual check up—making it a treat, not a chore—then we have her picture taken and go out for a special lunch.

Tara Vreeland, Princeton, N.J.

Birthday Clubs

Some retail chains sponsor birthday clubs that send you a coupon to use at birthday time when you register with them. Baskin-Robbins sends club "members" a coupon for a free single-scoop cone and a coupon worth $2 off on a birthday cake for kids up to age 12. At Sears Portrait Studio you'll receive a card one month prior to your birthday, good for a free 8" x 10" portrait. Many local restaurants have unadvertised Birthday Clubs. Ask for information and join up!

Birthday Books

Birthday-related books are available for children of all ages. They are always fun to read, especially near the big day. Almost every series has a birthday book from the *Spot* books by Eric Hill to the *Arthur* books by Marc Brown.

One-Minute Birthday Stories by Shari Lewis and Lan O'Kun (BDD 1995) has 20 stories, original and classic.

Dear Happy Birthday Duck by Eve Bunting, illus. Jan Brett (Houghton-Mifflin 1991) where everyone brings a gift.

Some Birthday! by Patricia Pollacco (Simon & Schuster 1991) is about a little girl and her father who only seems to forget her birthday.

Hector's New Sneakers by Amanda Vesey (Viking 1993) isn't what Hector had in mind for his birthday present.

Ask at your library or children's bookstore for suggestions.

What About the Rest of the Family on Party Days?

The birthday child is definitely the star; this is one day for letting your child indulge in pure narcissism. However, as the party planner, you will want to consider the rest of your family, too.

Siblings

Parties can be a natural source of jealousy for the kids who are not the center of attention. Watching a sibling in the limelight is not easy. Many children misbehave to get their share of attention. Giving them some special attention can help avoid disaster.

• Some say you should give a small gift to siblings, especially if younger, to avoid jealousy. Others say, don't—that siblings must learn that this is the birthday child's day and that they will have their own day when it's their time.

• Arrange for a younger sibling(s) and younger sibling(s) of the birthday child's friends to play together in a separate place, perhaps supervised by a helper hired to keep them occupied.

• Get out photos and memorabilia from a sibling's party. In addition to rediscovering some party ideas, you might convince the jealous child that his or her birthday was celebrated just as wholeheartedly as his or her sibling's.

• Perhaps an older sibling may prefer to come to the party as a guest, ringing the front doorbell (or possibly even under an assumed name!).

• Let an older sibling invite a guest, too, and put them in charge of announcing games, teaching songs, or helping serve food.

• Make plans to keep a younger sibling occupied and tended. Hire a baby sitter, neighbor child or ask Grandma to come and be in charge of him or her (if that's Grandma's style).

Pet Protection

Do get your pets out of the way for the party. You may prevent a disaster involving either the pet, a child, or both.

• Take your dog or cat out to the groomer for trimming, bathing, shots, whatever, or to the kennel for the day of the party. Or let your pet visit an animal-loving neighbor.

• Shut your pets in the basement or laundry room if they won't be miserable there and howl or bark.

• Put fish, turtles, or hamsters in a closed room where they won't attract the attention of children too young to handle them safely.

Special Occasion Birthdays

If your child's birthday falls on a holiday like Thanksgiving, New Year's, Halloween, or Valentine's Day, it can actually be helpful when deciding on a theme or decorations. If the birthday falls on or near a gift-giving holiday such as Christmas or Chanukah, your child may feel shortchanged in both attention and gifts. You might decorate one room just for the birthday or plan to give the party before or after the holiday. If the birthday falls on that once-in-four-years day, February 29, you'll have some serious explaining to do!

Birthdays On or Near a Gift-Giving Holiday

• If the birthday comes before the holiday, put up the holiday decorations on the birthday. If it occurs after the holiday, take down the holiday decorations and redecorate (lavishly!).

• Plan a neighborhood "birthday cake breakfast". Kids love the novelty of being allowed to eat cake in the morning. Schedule the children's birthday party one week later.

• Try to keep the birthday a separate celebration by choosing party themes and activities *not* related to the holiday.

• Schedule the birthday party before or after the holiday to keep it completely separate from the holiday.

• Plan a party at your child's preschool or school after the holiday recess to focus the birthday festivity away from the holiday atmosphere of the house.

• For a 4-year-old and over, having the birthday party out of the house helps separate the celebrations, but don't make it a given. Let there also be parties on the home front!

• Consider a "Twelfth Day" party for a birthday late in December or early January. The theme is based on the old favorite, "The Twelve Days of Christmas".

• Let your child be "King or Queen for the Day" to emphasize his or her special day separate from whatever is going on in the house for the holiday.

• Have a T-shirt made for your child that says something like, "It's My Birthday Today!" to be worn the entire day.

• Do *not* combine presents! "This gift is for your birthday *and* Christmas" can be disappointing, no matter how grand the gift is. Wrap birthday presents in birthday paper, *not* Christmas or Chanukah gift paper.

• Plan your budget far enough ahead so the holiday and birthday bills coming at the same time won't be overwhelming.

• Plan a half-birthday celebration during the summer (a picnic or back yard barbecue perhaps), with or without presents. It would be a good opportunity to use the "grab bag" idea—each child brings one present, each takes one home.

• Remember to greet your child with "Happy Birthday!" before you say "Merry Christmas," "Happy Chanukah," or whatever. It's surprisingly easy to forget!

Minimizing Midsummer Birthday Blues

The June-July-August birthday presents it own set of problems. Many children are away on vacation or in camp; there is no school class to bring cupcakes to; and the scarce party population makes for a limited number of presents. You might consider moving your child's birthday party ahead six months and plan a half-birthday celebration during the school year.

• Ask friends and relatives to cooperate by saving their cards and presents for the half-birthday celebration.

• On the half-birthday party day make two cakes and save the second cake in the freezer to enjoy on the actual birthday. Birthday cake will celebrate the day without a party or gifts.

• Many schools will celebrate half-birthdays—check it out

Parties for Two

Most parents of twins celebrate with a single party—few can handle two separate parties within a day or two. There are other reasons for joint parties—cousins or good friends whose birthdays fall on the same day or very close together. If it's a very busy time of year, sharing a party can be easier on the party planners and often easier on the pocketbook (savings on things like decorations and prizes, etc.). But be sure to have *two cakes*—very important!

• Invite guests both children know and children who know each other just as you would for an individual party.

• Seat the birthday children at opposite ends or on opposite sides of the table and bring the cakes in separately so the guests can sing "Happy Birthday" to each child individually and so each birthday child can blow out his or her candles.

• Ask that guests bring a present for both children, not just one to be shared. This may be a bit awkward, but you can tactfully tell one or two parents and ask them to pass the message along.

• Make one part of the party special for each child—perhaps a special game for one, a special activity for the other.

• Have separate gift-opening ceremonies so that each child can be the center of attention.

Chapter 10

Party Themes

Party supply stores and catalogs offer many items featuring the current media fads, but using some of the following ideas may be helpful planning a party just as successfully.

Backyard Beach Party

A summer or warm climate special, the beach party theme adds extra fun to a backyard party. It can be as filled with activities as the age of the children permits. Advise parents that children should bring towels and bathing suits (or wear them under their play clothes). The party can be given by a pool or not.

- *Refreshments*: Peanut butter sandwiches are fun cut into fish shapes. Serve Ants-on-a-Log (raisins on cream cheese in celery sticks), lemonade, snow cones, a cake with a smiley face. Serve lunch on a Frisbee® (lined with a paper plate) to take home. Spread blankets or beach towels on the grass or use lawn chairs for eating picnic-style.

- *Favors*: Sandbox toys for the children to play with at the party and then take home (buy different colors and use markers to label them with the children's names); bubble-blowing jars; plastic sunglasses; beach balls; paper mini-beach umbrellas.

- *Activities*: Sandbox or sand-pile play; splashing in a wading pool; running through the sprinkler, or jumping over the stream of water from a hose; finger painting or other arts and crafts;

water balloon toss; chalk drawing on the sidewalk. Searching for hidden seashells. (Define areas for games on the grass with flour; cleanup is easy with a hose off!)

• *Games:* Place some loose marbles in the bottom of a large tub and fill with water. Each child puts one bare foot into the tub, trying to lift the marbles to place them on the ground with his or her toes. Allot a specific amount of time (about one minute). Whoever has picked up the most marbles is the winner!

• *Variation:* A teddy bear or stuffed animal picnic—everyone brings their favorite teddy bear or animal friend.

Backyard Snow Party

You'll want to serve refreshments indoors, but extremely cold temperatures or a blizzard could interfere with outdoor play, so have alternate plans for indoor activities. Let the parents know that the children should wear warm, waterproof outer clothing.

• *Decorations*: Cutout paper snowflakes hung from the ceiling, a snowman centerpiece made of styrofoam balls.

• *Refreshments*: Ice cream balls to resemble snowballs; hot cocoa with mini-marshmallows.

• *Favors*: Sandbox pails and shovels for snow play; inexpensive plastic sleds (remember some rope for pulling).

• *Activities*: Give kids spray bottles filled with colored water (a drop of food coloring) and let them "paint" snow sculptures they have make. Get the group together to make a huge snowman. Go sledding. Play a game called *Pie*: shovel a big circle path through the snow; then shovel paths to divide the circle into quarters; the children play tag while staying on the snow paths.

Circus or Carnival Party

Lots of balloons, helium or otherwise, and clown hats may be enough to make 3-year-olds happy; older kids can handle and appreciate more excitement.

• *Invitations*: Blow up a balloon, write party information on it, let the air out and mail it in an envelope; place an animal-shaped note in an animal cracker box, or design the invitation to look like a ticket to the circus or carnival.

• *Decorations*: If it's an outdoor party you can get the feel of the "Big Top" by using a camping canopy, available at sporting goods store, and relatively inexpensive. Use lots of balloons, some can be fastened to sticks stuck in the ground to mark the path to the front door. Indoors use circus posters and a "big top" swag of crepe paper streamers hung over the table or in the party room. Decorate the cake with plastic circus animals or frosted animal crackers. Striped straws with small pennant flags taped to one end can be used in various ways. A clown doll holding a balloon bouquet can be a fun centerpiece idea.

• *Refreshments*: Set up a decorated "refreshment stand" from which you serve hot dogs wrapped in paper, sodas in paper cups and bags of peanuts and popcorn. Other ideas: clown-face sandwiches (page 54); popcorn balls; clown ice cream cones (a pointed cone looks like a hat when set upsidedown on top of a scoop of ice cream decorated with candies as a face); a slice of ice cream on a plate becomes a circus wagon when pretzel rounds or cookies are added for wheels and animal crackers are placed in front to pull. Freeze animal shaped chewy fruit snacks in ice cubes. Serve "Monkey Munch" (made from various dried cereals, nuts, trail mix and banana chips) or a clown-face pizza (pepperoni eyes, chopped tomato hair, and sausage slice mouth).

• *Favors*: Clown hats, balloons formed into animal shapes, whistles, hula hoops, boxes of animal crackers, circus coloring books, small stuffed or plastic animal figures.

• *Activities*: For 5 and 6 -year-olds, a clown who has been hired to face paint the children or to entertain; a peanut hunt; making clown hats; drawing clown faces on paper plates; musical chairs to circus music; walking a tight rope (masking tape in a straight line on the floor); *Pin the Nose on the Clown*; a circus parade march with toy musical instruments or stuffed animals, accompanied by circus music.

Sports Theme Party

If your child is interested in a particular sport—soccer, T-ball, baseball, etc.—you might hire a high school student "coach" to organize a game. Use a green (turf) table covering, ball-park type foods, team "stuff." This party is very popular with kids, especially boys, and requires less work for the parents.

• *Refreshments*: Birthday cakes can be shaped and decorated to resemble footballs, bats, soccer balls, etc. Make popcorn or Rice Krispie® "baseballs." Serve Cracker Jack boxes.

• *Favors*: Paper megaphones, miniature sports equipment, pennants, T-shirts, mugs, visors or baseball caps.

Dress-Up Party

A dress-up party does not have to be only for girls—little boys love to dress up, too! Set out a big dress-up box of collected clothes, hats, gloves, jewelry, etc. You can buy inexpensive black top hats and bow ties. You can ask parents to send along contributions to the box (old costumes of any kind are great), which can be returned after the party. Be sure to provide a full-length mirror!

• *Decorations*: Create a centerpiece of stacked-up hats of all kinds to use in the dress-up.

• *Refreshments*: Serve beverages in plastic wine glasses, finger sandwiches cut into fancy shapes, "cocktail" weiners, "hors d'oeuvres" made of cheese cubes, fruit, or pieces of meat stuck with fancy frilled toothpicks, and any other fancy canapes you can make. Serve them at a formal-looking table.

• *Favors*: Instant photos of the children in their dress-up outfits, perfume samples, jewelry, small purses, hats, bow ties, canes, inexpensive makeup (lipstick and eye shadow a must!).

• *Activities*: Videotape the children after they're dressed up and let them watch the video before they leave. Craft activities might include: making hats using sequins, lace, fabric scraps, etc. glued to paper plates or folded newspaper; making jewelry; putting on makeup and nail polish; drawing on beards and mustaches, eyebrows and goatees; making and decorating paper bow ties. Let the children wear their creations home.

Doll's Tea Party

The doll tea party is a much-loved, traditional party. Little girls won't need many decorative props to set the scene but older girls appreciate lots of elaborate details. Some girls like sharing their dolls with their friends; others prefer to keep their treasure all to themselves. Greet each guest formally as "Ms. So-and-So."

• *Decorations*: Set a doll's tea table with miniature dishes and food; the guests' table could resemble a tearoom set with pretty china, flowers and candles—the fancier the better!.

• *Refreshments*: Tiny finger sandwiches (peanut butter is fine) cut in dainty shapes, decorated petit fours, ice cream balls cut with a melon scoop. Serve very weak, sweetened tea, ginger ale, or fruit juice from teacups, the prettier the better.

• *Favors*: Dollhouse furniture, doll clothes, and accessories.

• *Activities*: Playing house with dolls, sewing doll clothes you've cut out in advance.

• *Variations*: Stuffed animal or teddy bear party; dress them up with scarves, ribbons, etc.

Frontier or Western Party

The West and its traditions still appeals to many different aged children. They can come dressed in blue jeans, western style shirts, cowboy boots, and hats (or give hats as favors).

• *Decorations*: Homemade Native American drums; bales of hay set out as seats outside or in the garage. A tent set up in the yard (or even indoors) as a campsite. Lasso ropes. Paper cutout cactus shapes as placemats or for wall or room decorations.

• *Refreshments*: Roast hot dogs on a stick over a grill and top with chili if you like; buffalo wings; serve beverages from coffee tins or mugs. If you're campers, some of your camping gear (mess kit for dishes, camp coffee pot for pouring the drinks) on a red-checked tablecloth adds an atmosphere of "roughing it."

• *Favors*: Bandanas, water pistols, beef jerky, small toy figures of cowboys and horses. Name tags cut out of cardboard (or sugar cookies) shaped as five-star sheriff badges.

• *Activities*: Water guns to shoot out candle flames; *Duck, Duck, Goose* (page 103) played around a campfire (made by cutting cardboard "logs" and using rocks to encircle the logs); sing cowboy songs or play any musical game to western music—

Musical Stagecoach is a variation of *Musical Chairs* simply set to western music. Take photos against a western background and put them in a "Outlaw Wanted" frame. Watch the video "Cowboy Days", "So You Want to be a Cowboy" or similar title (available from Tapeworm Video Distributors, (805) 257-4904, $14.95) for footage of real cowboys riding horses and rounding up cattle, and sing-along campfire songs.

Pirate Party

Little kids love the wicked, swashbuckling atmosphere of a pirate party. Give each child a bandana and an eye patch as they arrive. Consider reading a favorite pirate story to them while they eat.

• *Invitation*: Hand-deliver a treasure map (to your house) tucked into a bottle, with the child's name on the back of the map.

• *Decorations*: Hang skull-and-crossbones flags or use them as place mats; use black crepe paper streamers and balloons, and lots of tin foil.

• *Refreshments*: Chicken legs, potato chips, a square or oblong two-layer treasure chest cake, decorated with jelly bean jewels and candy gold coins; or a cake with a "treasure" of candy hidden in each piece; a red drink such as cranberry juice or a blend of cranberry and orange juice.

• *Favors*: Black eye patches, fake mustaches or beards, scarves, bandanas, small bags filled with gold coin candies or new shiny pennies; swords cut from cardboard.

• *Activities:* A treasure hunt using a single map for everyone and a shared treasure, or individual maps and separate treasures; fishing for gold coin candies which have been sunk in a treasure chest (page 112 *Fishing for Favors* game).

Backwards Party

Preschoolers and kindergartners are old enough to enjoy the concept of turning everything around backwards. Invitations can be printed in mirror writing; the children asked to come with their clothes worn upside down, inside out, or backwards; entering the house by the back door and being greeted with "good-bye," just to get things started off "wrong." (Don't forget to wish the guests "Hello" as they leave.)

• *Decorations*: Balloons and streamers tied underneath tables and chairs; posters and other decorations hung upside down. Spread the tablecloth on the floor under the table, and have the children sit on the floor around it for the refreshments.

• *Refreshments*: Serve the meal in backwards order, which means the birthday cake and ice cream first! Give the children juice or soda in cans opened at the wrong ends, frost the cake on the bottom, use candles that re-light when they're blown out; serve inside-out sandwiches made with the bread inside meat or cheese slices.

• *Favors*: Left-handed articles. Favors wrapped with gift paper turned inside out.

• *Activities*: Give prizes before the game (making sure each child gets one), then play any noncompetitive games backwards: *Pin the Donkey on the Tail, Backwards Relay Races, Bean Bag Toss* with the children throwing bean bags backwards (behind them over their shoulders). Play word games such as having each child write down (backwards) as many words as possible using the letters in "y-a-d-h-t-r-i-B y-p-p-a-H." Winners are losers, and losers become winners; use your imagination to create games or activities that reflect a topsy-turvy format. Let the children help you think !

Color Party

Use your child's favorite color as the party theme. For example, all red invitations, decorations, frosting on the cake, drinks, etc.. Have the birthday child and all the guests dress in red, and ask them to bring a red present (wrapped in red paper, of course). Red favors such as coloring books and red crayons or markers.

Artist's Party

Children are naturally creative. What better way to let their imaginations soar than with an artist's party?

• *Invitations*: Museum shops sell inexpensive artistic postcards. Or design your own invitation fashioned to resemble a paint brush decorated with a splotch of paint, "Artist's Party" and the rest of the party information in bright colors.

• *Decorations*: Decorate the room with lots of color. Put a sign that says, "Art Gallery" or "Artist's Loft" on the door to the party room. Use a palette, brushes and paints as a centerpiece.

• *Refreshments*: Fashion the cake in the shape of an artist's palette. Better yet, let the children "paint" the cake!

• *Favors*: Markers, crayons, pastels, paint sets with extra brushes sketch books and play dough or modeling clay.

• *Activities*: As the kids arrive let them work on a giant mural. Ask each guest to bring a plain white T-shirt to decorate (page 87). Provide paper, stickers, glitter, etc. for them to make their own stationery; add boxes and ribbons to make gift sets. Let the children build sculptures with bits and pieces you have on hand—strips of wood, cardboard, beads, old jewelry, glitter, cork, buttons, ribbons, etc. Be sure to have lots of glue, scissors and markers. Or provide play dough or clay to sculpt. Try no-mess finger painting: put a few spoonfuls of liquid paint into a Ziploc® bag (make sure you zip it closed!), and let the children finger paint by creating designs with fingers against the plastic. Hang a sheet over a clothesline and let the kids spray paint it with spray bottles of food coloring or water colors. Play music and ask the children to paint a picture of the feeling the music arouses. Photocopy favorite cartoons for the children to color.

Prehistoric Dinosaur Party

You don't have to go far these days to find dinosaur items and activities. It appears that the dinosaur craze is here to stay!

• *Decorations*: Draw dinosaurs on paper plates, cut them out and use a paper punch to make holes at both top and bottom; thread a straw through the holes for a drinking straw decoration. A child's name written on the dinosaur turns the decoration into a place card. Plastic eggs become dinosaurs eggs to use as table decorations. A table centerpiece can be made by shaping defrosted bread dough into a dinosaur shape (clip the dough on top to make a spiny back), baking and decorating. Attach a helium balloon with ribbon to a stuffed or blown-up dinosaur toy. Arrange a rock pie on the table decorated with enough small plastic dinosaurs for each child to take home.

• *Refreshments*: Dinosaur cookie cutters can be used on thin slices of cheese, or for sandwiches. Serve "dinosaur teeth" (candy corn), "prehistoric punch" (make sure the name doesn't reflect the age of the drink), "brontosaurus burgers" and "dino-sundaes." Dinosaur trail mix can include pieces of dinosaur-shaped cereal.

• *Favors*: Children's museum gift stores and most toy stores are good sources for prehistoric paraphernalia. Books or coloring books featuring dinosaurs are always popular, as are stickers. Plastic or rubber toy dinosaurs are readily available .

• *Activities*: Have a *Dinosaur Race (Wheelbarrow Race)*. Arrange a *Dinosaur Hunt*: hide small dinosaur toys or eggs or cutout paper dinosaur "bones"—or dog biscuit bones. *Disappearing Dinosaurs* is a reverse *Hide and Seek*: the person who is "It" is the one who hides—the rest of the children look for the one who hid. One by one the "dinosaurs" disappear. The last one to find the group is "It" next time. Pre-record a Flintstones TV show (not *Jurrasic Park*!) to play on your VCR as a quiet activity before the children go home.

Fairy Tale Party

Fairy tales *can* come true (or at least to life) at birthday parties! You might even hire a "Good Fairy" to help you run the activities.

• *Invitations*: Add confetti or glitter to the invitation envelope.

• *Decorations*: Scatter confetti in a path leading to the party room, telling the children they're "fairy footprints." Make a gumdrop tree outdoors by hanging small bags of gumdrops on tree branches using ornament hooks. Create an outdoor fairy-land garden out of cardboard toadstools, giant paper flowers, etc. attached to garden stakes. Hang tinsel-tied balloons, gum-drops, or twinkling Christmas lights. Decorate paper crowns with tinsel for the children to wear.

• *Refreshments*: Sandwiches cut with cookie cutters into hearts, stars, butterflies or flowers. Pink lemonade. Hide a jellybean in one of the "Jack-in-the-Beanstalk" cupcakes; whoever finds it gets a prize. Frost a sheet cake with a rainbow and add a "pot of gold" (a small cup, spray painted and filled with foil-covered chocolate candy coins). Make a "Veggie Magic Wand"—a celery stick filled with cream cheese or peanut butter and topped with a cheese star (use a cookie cutter).

• *Favors*: Little bags of "fairy dust" (gold and silver glitter). Fairy skirts made of from nylon netting: gather two-yard pieces lengthwise and sew ribbon over one edge as a waistband, tie around each "fairy" guest. Make Magic Wands from tall straws taped with a star and Christmas tinsel ribbons. Make (or let the children make) Tooth Fairy bags which could range from a little velvet drawstring bag to a lace trimmed pocket. Add a small travel toothbrush or a quarter to each finished bag that is taken home as a favor.

• *Activities:* Fish in a "pot of gold" for small prizes: use a large flowerpot spray-painted gold or covered with gold foil and placed at the end of a cardboard rainbow. Ask someone to be a helper and make sure each child hooks a prize. Choose your child's favorite fairy tale and read it aloud or have the children act it out—the birthday child gets the starring role, of course! Make construction paper crowns for each child. Have a hunt for Cinderella's Slipper by hiding a pretty high-heeled shoe. (Show the children its mate so they know what to look for.) Rent *Cinderella, Snow White, Aladdin* or one of the other popular fairy tale movies now available on video. Play *Musical Chairs* to the music, "Twinkle, Twinkle Little Star."

Rainbow Connection Party

There is nothing prettier or more upbeat than a rainbow theme for a birthday party, especially for younger children.

• *Invitations*: Let the birthday child draw and color rainbows on the invitations with markers. Ask the guests to come dressed in their favorite primary-colored clothes.

• *Decorations*: Place a rainbow arch over the front door or hang rainbow streamers from the door frame for the guests to walk through. (In case you've forgotten, the order of colors of the rainbow: red, orange, yellow, green, blue, indigo, violet.) For background music, play the Muppets' "Rainbow Connection."

• *Refreshments*: Serve a multicolored layered birthday cake (page 46). Rainbow layered Jell-O® in parfait glasses is easy to prepare and always impressive. Serve the refreshments on a variety of brightly colored paper plates, napkins and cups. Serve Neapolitan ice cream or ice cream balls in several colors.

• *Favors*: There are many inexpensive items featuring rainbows, such as pencils, magnets and stickers. Glass prisms, kaleidoscopes and crayons or markers in primary colors are interesting and usually inexpensive to give.

• *Activities*: Draw and color rainbows with markers on white helium balloons. Play *Color Bingo* or *Pin the Rainbow on the Pot of Gold*. Plan a treasure hunt that will end (naturally) with a prize at the pot of gold. For a quiet activity, assign each guest a color, give them a stack of magazines and ask them to cut out anything of that color and paste the pictures on to a sheet of paper. At the end of the party gather all the sheets and fasten them together to make a rainbow book for the birthday child.

Space Travel Party

Space travel remains fascinating for children even though it has moved out of the realm of fantasy and into reality. Popular television shows or movies like *Star Trek* or *Star Wars* are easy and fun themes to plan the party around.

• *Decorations*: Use lots of silver and blue balloons. White, twinkling Christmas lights give a starlight effect to a room or ceiling. Hang paper stars and moons, hunks of fiberfill clouds or spray-painted styrofoam ball planets by string or clear fishing line from the ceiling. Play background music from *Star Wars*, *Star Trek* or *2001*. Rocks spray-painted silver with the guests' names written in permanent black marker can be used as placecards on the table. Slightly scrunched-up aluminum foil makes for a celestial tablecloth. An empty paper towel roll covered with aluminum foil forms the body of a rocket ship.

• *Refreshments*: Serve "freeze-dried space food" like beef jerky, dried fruits, nuts and raisins, or real freeze-dried foodstuffs you can buy at any outdoor camping or surplus store. Bake cupcakes and decorate them with tiny American flags on picks. Use bright sparklers on the birthday cake instead of candles.

• *Favors*: Activity or comic books with a space theme, Milky Way™ candy bars, toy spaceships and travelers, wraparound sunglass "visors," space creature erasers, glow-in-the-dark stars.

• *Activities*: Be creative with games like *Hot Asteroid* (Hot Potato), *Astronaut's Bluff* (Blindman's Bluff with spaceship sounds), or *Moon Walk* (Hopscotch). Hide individually foil-wrapped bags of peanuts for a *Moon Rock Hunt*. Have the children write about themselves on small cards, place the cards in a tin can " time capsule;" let the children bury it in the back yard. Decorate a large discarded refrigerator or appliance box as a space ship (be sure to include a control panel on the inside). Play the memory game "I'm going to the moon and I'm going to take a___with me;" each child adding an item to the list after repeating what was previously said. Sing "One Little, Two Little, Three Little Astronauts." Make "moon people" by drawing faces on half of a L'Eggs® egg-shaped container and using clip clothespins for legs. Watch the video "Someday I Wanna Be An Astronaut" (Bell Canyon, 1-800-335-3133, for ages 3-8).

Hawaiian Luau Party

What is more fun and festive than a Hawaiian Party?

- *Decorations*: Hang fishnets from the ceiling. Have big shells, strings of shells, real or fake flowers, and driftwood on tables or on the floor. Hang Polynesian travel posters. Use straw placemats on the table. Bring all your plants into one room to create a tropical look. Cut palm trees and a sun out of cardboard and decorate the walls. Use an old trunk as a "treasure chest" to hold the gifts. If it's wintertime, turn up the thermostat and encourage the guests to wear summer play clothes or even swim suits. Decorate with colorful beach towels.

- *Refreshments*: Hawaiian Punch or a homemade blend of pineapple juice and ginger ale served in plastic margarita glasses. Fruit can be served from a scooped-out pineapple, cantaloupe or watermelon. Make assorted kabobs of cubed cheese, lunch meats, fruits and pickles. Or make a kabob out of just fruits and serve with a bowl of yogurt dip alongside.

- *Favors*: Make candy leis by tying pieces of wrapped candy together with ribbons. Straw hats or visors can be birthday hats. A small flowering or cactus plant can be a take-home gift. Shells filled with small candies, nuts or raisins can be wrapped with plastic wrap and tied up with a ribbon.

- *Activities*: Make grass skirts out of crepe paper strips or strips cut from a large green plastic garbage bag. Or make a skirt by wrapping a green sheet of crepe around the waist and cutting fringes from the bottom hem up to the waist. Play Hawaiian music and dance the hula or play *Musical Chairs*. Weave placemats out of paper strips. Make leis of Life Savers® strung on licorice strings. Make tissue paper flowers. Set up sandbox play or art projects. Devise a sea shell toss.

Zoo or Safari Party

An exotic animal party appeals to both boys and girls and lends itself to many variations.

• *Decorations*: Make cages for small stuffed animals using shoe boxes cut open on one side with straws for cage bars. Decorate the cake with inexpensive plastic animals or animal crackers. Use crepe paper strips to make bars at room entrances. Ask the children to bring large stuffed animals and set them at the table or keep them together in a corner marked "Petting Zoo." Play animal sound tapes as background "music."

• *Refreshments*: What else but animal fare? Label a dish of fish crackers "Seal Supper," plate of bananas "Monkey Meal," a plate of peanuts "Elephant Eats." Animal crackers are a must. Critter cupcakes are frosted and decorated with various candies, coconut and raisins for faces and ears or topped with miniature plastic animals. Use animal cookie cutters to cut sandwiches. Make a tiger cake: 9" round layer cake, two cupcake ears, orange frosting with chocolate syrup stripes, eyes, mouth and teeth. Or a snake cake: an angel food cake cut horizontally in thirds, vertically in half; the half-circles arranged alternately in a serpentine design, frosted with green tinted whipped cream and decorated with grape "eyes," set on a bed of lettuce leaves "grass."

• *Favors*: Wrap small stuffed animals with crepe paper strips, forming a ball as you wind; tape small favors to the crepe paper. Inexpensive plastic animals, windup creatures, animal stickers, balloon animals, bags of peanuts or animal crackers.

• *Activities*: Make "snakes": stuff old neckties, widowed socks or cut pantyhose legs with rag strips or old nylons, sew on string tongues and button eves. draw skin patterns with broad markers. Make "lions": use markers to draw lion faces on yellow paper plates, add manes of yarn pieces glued around the plates' edges. Play animal charades by having the children act out animals for the others to guess. Paint animal faces on each child. Make safari hats out of decorated paper plates and string. Have an *Elephant Hunt* (for hidden peanuts) or a *Banana-Eating Race* (page 108 *African Safari*). Play "*Polly Parrot*" (*Simon Says*) using animal movements like, "Swing your arms like an elephant trunk." Substitute wild animal names for *Duck, Duck, Grey Duck*. Plan an animal parade with the children carrying their stuffed animals as they march. Rent an age-appropriate movie, ranging from *Dumbo* to *Curious George* to *Born Free*. Read animal stories aloud as a quiet activity. And easiest of all, arrange for part or all of the party to be held at the local zoo!

Now it's time for you to get into action.
Have a wonderful party!

Index

BIRTHDAY PARTY MEMORY RECORD SHEET

CHILD _____   Birthdate _____

Age (circle)   1   2   3   4   5   6   7   8   9

Day of the Week _____ 19 __   Weather _____

Headlines of the Day:
_____
_____

Guests:
_____   _____
_____   _____
_____

Food/Favors/Theme:
_____
_____
_____

Games/Activites:
_____
_____
_____

Gifts Received:
_____   _____
_____   _____
_____   _____

BIRTHDAY PARTY MEMORY RECORD SHEET

CHILD _____ Birthdate _____

Age (circle) 1 2 3 4 5 6 7 8 9

Day of the Week _____ 19 ___ Weather _____

Headlines of the Day:
_____
_____

Guests:
_____   _____
_____   _____
_____   _____

Food/Favors/Theme:
_____
_____
_____

Games/Activites:
_____
_____
_____

Gifts Received:
_____   _____
_____   _____
_____   _____